Mediterranean Diet Cookbook for Beginners

Flavorful Recipes to Unveil the
Secrets of a Healthy Lifestyle

Angela Sherman

Author's Message

Before you start reading, I would like to thank you all and each for taking the time to read my cookbook.

It means a lot to me that out of thousands other books you've chosen mine.

In this cookbook, I tried to incorporate my experience with my knowledge and I tried my best not only to make this guide useful but also simple to read for anyone.

Each reader is my friend who is valuable to me.

TABLE OF CONTENTS

Introduction

The Mediterranean region is abundant in plenty of fruits, vegetables, nuts, a variety of dairy products, and delicious fish. The people of that region are known for their positive outlook, excellent health, and longevity. The Mediterranean diet has gained popularity over the years as a healthy eating plan that encompasses the best food habits of the region. Over the last few years, it has been consistently ranked as the number one diet by U.S. News and World Reports.

People worldwide choose the Mediterranean diet for its numerous benefits, including dynamic weight loss, increased stamina, lowered cholesterol levels, and reduced risks of cancer, metabolic syndrome, and type 2 diabetes. The Mediterranean diet is a lifestyle that was created originated in Greece, Italy, Croatia, Turkey, Africa, and other countries in that region. This well-balanced diet is easy to follow and doesn't require you to give up the food you love. At the same time, it helps to maintain the right intake of calories and macros.

Nutritionists worldwide are increasingly recommending the Mediterranean diet as the best approach to support overall health. This eating plan doesn't have strict rules about how much food you should consume during the day, and it allows you to listen to your body's needs. The well-balanced, plant-based meals minimize the chances of overeating. However, this can also be a challenge for individuals dealing with obesity.

This cookbook includes the best, the most popular, and the most delightful recipes of the Mediterranean diet. The recipes have been carefully selected, and ingredients have been adjusted to be easily found in the nearest supermarket. Whether you're a beginner or an experienced cook, this cookbook will serve as a valuable guide.

Benefits of the Mediterranean diet

The Mediterranean diet is a unique diet that can be your lifestyle. It has numerous health benefits which you haven't even expected.

- Reduces the symptoms of popular diseases: such as cancer, type 2 diabetes, Alzheimer's disease, Parkinson's disease, and multiple sclerosis.

- Improves men's and women's health: the diet increases sperm quality, enhance natural fertility, which reduces the need for vitro fertilization (IVF).

- Improves general body health: lowers the bad cholesterol, decreases inflammation, increases healthy gut bacteria, supports the immune system, regulates the blood sugar level, and recovers the damaged cells and tissues.

- Weight control: the diet helps to manage and control the weight and stimulate the body to lose weight.

- Preventing and fights with skin problems: the diet helps to balance hormones which lead to acne reduction. The diet also helps to fight oily and dry skin, as well as wrinkles.

- Longer lifespan: some of the studies have shown that following the Mediterranean diet helps you live longer and most importantly healthier.

To sum up, the right and permanent following of the Mediterranean diet can lead to gorgeous results, which can be seen both inside and outside.

What to eat?

The Mediterranean diet demands a balanced combination of vegetables and fruits, the right fats, legumes, and dairy in daily meals. This plant-based diet will be very easy and useful for you if you figure out the list of allowed food and implement it in your diet.

It doesn't have a strict list of food to eat. However, there are some general recommendations that you should follow to achieve visible results.

- Vegetables: as it is a plant-based diet, all types of vegetables are allowed, including leafy greens.
- Fruits and berries: all types of fresh fruits and berries are allowed.
- Nuts and seeds: chia seeds, almonds, pine nuts, pumpkin seeds, walnuts, sunflower seeds, sesame seeds, macadamia nuts, and peanuts.
- Tubers: sweet potato, turnip, radish, rutabaga.
- Legumes: all types of beans, legumes, and peas are allowed.
- Whole grains: barley, buckwheat, bulgur, corn, brown rice, cut oats, couscous, whole-grain bread.
- Fish and Seafood: calamari, anchovies, cod, mackerel, clams, crab, oysters, scallops, salmon, sardines, shrimp, lobster, tuna, trout, tilapia.
- Meat and poultry: white cuts of poultry such as skinless chicken and turkey; goat, and lamb.
- Dairy products: low-fat cheese such as brie, chevre, feta, halloumi, and mozzarella, low-fat yogurt such as Greek yogurt.
- Herbs and spices: all-natural spices.
- Beverages: coffee, tea, water, and red wine in moderation.
- Sauces and dressing: balsamic vinegar, apple cider vinegar, homemade pesto, tomato sauce, and tzatziki.

What to avoid?

The Mediterranean diet is aimed to help you prioritize the healthy source of calories you consume per day. It can help you not only with weight loss but also teaches you to eat healthy.

This is a list of foods that should be limited while dieting due to their harmful effects on health and diet result. By doing that, you will help yourself to achieve the magnificent results that the Mediterranean diet promises.

- Sugars extras: such as tapioca syrup, corn syrup, cane sugar, caramel, agave syrup, and maple syrup.
- Beverages: soda, sports drinks, bottled coffee, tea drinks, smoothies, and alcohol mixers.
- Dessert and sweets: all sweets and desserts with added sugar such as sugar-coated nuts, candies, ice cream, sweet train mixes, pastries, cakes, muffins, sugary cereals, and dried fruits such as prunes.
- Dairy: full-fat milk, chocolate milk, milkshake, whipped cream toppings.
- Meat and poultry: processed meat and poultry, chicken and turkey skin, processed sausages, bacon, and ham.
- Sauces and dressings: sugar-added and high-sodium sauces, dressings, and marinades.

Cooking tips

1 Swap red meat for lean proteins such as fish and poultry. They are rich in vitamins and minerals such as iron. Also, they are good sources of proteins. Such food provides vital nutrients for our skin and muscles. However, poultry and seafood should be in moderation while dieting.

2 Swaps cakes with fresh fruits or dried fruits like apricots, cherries, or figs. They are a nutrient powerhouse. It is an amazing source of fiber, antioxidants, and C vitamin. Make the fruits visible at home and grab some with you for work, so you can eat them in case your stomach starts growling.

3 Right consumption of eggs and dairy products. Eating such food in moderation will help lower the risk of diabetes, metabolic syndrome, obesity, and cardiovascular diseases.

4 More water. You can get extra calories via drinks which is bad. Such beverages as margaritas or wine are high caloric and you will simply stay hungry.

5 Enjoy every bite. The Mediterranean diet is more about lifestyle but not about dieting. Eat your food slowly, and feel the taste of every bite. Instead of eating your meal in front of the TV, make it on your patio or together with friends and family. It will help you to eat slowly as a result consume less but stay full.

6 Only high-quality food. You should always read the labels on the food you buy. If you are not sure about the nutritional info or the info you read is unclear – better avoid this product. Buying food in supermarkets is still okay but do it in a smart way. Choose local farmers' production or food which is organic. Find the farmer's markets in your area and make purchases there.

7 Use only extra virgin olive oil as a primary cooking oil. It will help you to avoid harmful fats like butter.

8 Avoid fast foods and processed foods. Sometimes it can be tough; however, you can always change such food with homemade.

9 Focus on fruits, vegetables, whole grains, and beans. They are at the very bottom of the Mediterranean pyramid and are the base of the diet. A good portion of greens salad will satisfy your hunger. Such food will make you feel healthier. Moreover, a diet that is rich in fruits and vegetables can lower the risk of heart disease and stroke. Scientists prove that they have a positive effect on the level of blood sugar too.

10 Nuts for snacks. Nuts such as cashews, almonds, and pistachios are a good idea for on-to-go snacks. Scientists proved that swapping standard snacks like chips and cookies for nuts helps to lower "empty" calories, sugars, and sodium.

BREAKFAST RECIPES

INGREDIENTS

- 2 bell peppers, chopped
- 3 beefsteak tomatoes, peeled, chopped
- 1 teaspoon olive oil
- 1 jalapeno pepper, chopped
- 2 eggs, beaten

Menemen

 10 mins   15 mins   2

METHODS

O1 Pour the olive oil into the skillet and add jalapeno pepper and bell peppers. Roast peppers for 3 minutes, then stir well.

O2 Add tomatoes and cook the mixture for 3 minutes more. Mash the mixture gently with the help of the fork and cook on low heat for 4 minutes more.

O3 Crack the eggs into the mixture and whisk well until everything is homogeneous.Cook the meal for an additional 4 minutes.

Nutritional Value

Calories: 78	Fat: 3.7	Carbs: 8.5
Fiber: 2	Sugar: 5.7	Protein: 4.2

INGREDIENTS

- 3 eggs
- 4 beefsteak tomatoes, peeled, chopped
- 1 tablespoon olive oil
- 1 sweet yellow pepper, chopped
- 1 white onion, diced
- 1 garlic clove, peeled, diced
- 1 teaspoon ground cumin
- 1 teaspoon ground paprika
- 2 oz fresh cilantro, chopped
- 1 oz fresh parsley, chopped

Shashuka

 10 mins   10 mins   3

METHODS

O1 Pour olive oil into the deep skillet and preheat well. Add sweet pepper, onion, and garlic. Cook the ingredients until they are soft.

O2 Throw in the tomatoes and cook the ingredients for 5 more minutes on medium heat. Sprinkle the mixture with ground cumin and paprika, then stir well.

O3 Crack the eggs into the tomato mixture and cook them for 3 additional minutes or until the egg whites are solid. Sprinkle the cooked shakshuka with cilantro and parsley.

Nutritional Value

Calories: 78	Fat: 3.7	Carbs: 8.5
Fiber: 2	Sugar: 5.7	Protein: 4.2

Egg Wrap

🕐 10 mins   🍲 10 mins   👤 3

INGREDIENTS

- 3 chicken fillets
- 3 corn tortillas
- 3 lettuce leaves
- 1 cup cherry tomatoes, halved
- ½ cup Greek yogurt
- 1 teaspoon dried basil
- 1 teaspoon minced garlic
- 1 teaspoon ground black pepper
- ½ teaspoon ground cumin
- 2 tablespoons olive oil
- 1 teaspoon ground turmeric

METHODS

01   Mix chicken fillets with ground black pepper, olive oil, and ground turmeric. Then, roast on medium-high heat for 4 minutes on each side.

02   Combine Greek yogurt with dried basil, minced garlic, and ground cumin. Spread the yogurt mixture evenly over the corn tortillas.

03   Put the lettuce leaves on top of the yogurt mixture. Add cooked chicken fillets and cherry tomatoes. Roll up the tortillas into the wraps.

Nutritional Value

Calories: 454   Fat: 21.8   Carbs: 15.9

Fiber: 2.7   Sugar: 3.2   Protein: 47.8

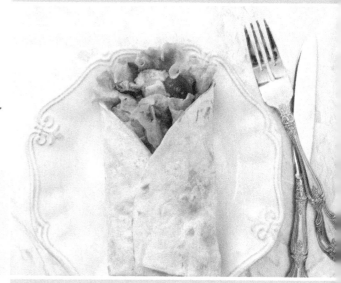

Basil Fried Egg

🕐 10 mins   🍲 8 mins   👤 1

INGREDIENTS

- 1 whole egg
- 1 oz fresh basil leaves
- 1 teaspoon olive oil
- 1 shallot onion, peeled, sliced
- 2 cherry tomatoes, halved
- 1 teaspoon black thyme

METHODS

01   Pour olive oil into the skillet and preheat well. Add shallot onion and cook it on medium heat until it is light brown. Throw in the fresh basil and stir the mixture well.

02   Crack the egg into the mixture of fried shallot onion and basil. Then, cook it for 3-4 minutes or until the egg is cooked.

03   Sprinkle the cooked egg with black thyme. Add cherry tomatoes as a garnish.

Nutritional Value

Calories: 154   Fat: 9.7   Carbs: 10.7

Fiber: 3.4   Sugar: 6.9   Protein: 8.6

INGREDIENTS

- 3 eggs, beaten
- 1 cup cherry tomatoes, halved
- 1 cup baby spinach leaves
- 2 oz goat cheese, crumbled
- 1 teaspoon olive oil
- 1 teaspoon sunflower seeds

Tender Omelet with Cherry Tomatoes

 10 mins 10 mins 2

METHODS

O1 Preheat olive oil in the skillet. Add beaten eggs and cook for 3 minutes per side.

O2 Transfer the cooked eggs to the serving plates. Top them with cherry tomatoes and goat cheese.

O3 Sprinkle the meal with the sunflower seeds. Place the fresh spinach leaves on the side of the cooked omelet.

Nutritional Value

Calories: 265	Fat: 19.5	Carbs: 5.3
Fiber: 1.5	Sugar: 3.6	Protein: 18.3

INGREDIENTS

- 4 eggs, beaten
- 1 tablespoon olive oil
- ¼ teaspoon ground black pepper
- 2 cups fresh arugula
- 1 English cucumber, peeled, sliced
- 3 tomatoes, roughly chopped
- 1 tablespoon canola oil

Breakfast Scramble

 10 mins 10 mins 3

METHODS

O1 Pour olive oil into the skillet and preheat. Add eggs and whisk until egg yolks and egg whites become homogeneous.

O2 Sprinkle the eggs with ground black pepper and cook the mixture for 3 minutes. Place the cooked scramble into the serving plates.

O3 Add the mix of fresh arugula, English cucumber, and tomatoes into the skillet and cook for 1 minute. Sprinkle the mixture with canola oil.

O4 Add cooked vegetable mixture to the scrumble.

Nutritional Value

Calories: 206	Fat: 15.6	Carbs: 9.5
Fiber: 2.2	Sugar: 5.6	Protein: 9.5

Oatmeal and Carrot Muffins

 10 mins   35 mins   4

METHODS

01 Mix all-purpose flour with baking powder, canola oil, grated carrot, oatmeal, Erythritol, and eggs until they are homogeneous.

02 Fill the muffin molds with the muffin batter and bake at 350°F for 35 minutes.

03 Cool the cooked muffins and top with blueberries and mint leaves.

Nutritional Value

Calories: 351	Fat: 19.1	Carbs: 34.8
Fiber: 2.9	Sugar: 2	Protein: 10.5

INGREDIENTS

- 1 cup all-purpose flour
- 1 teaspoon baking powder
- ¼ cup canola oil
- 1 carrot, grated
- ½ cup oatmeal
- ¼ cup Erythritol
- 4 eggs, beaten
- 1 oz mint leaves, for serving
- 1 oz blueberries, for serving

Zucchini Pancakes

 10 mins   20 mins   4

METHODS

01 In the mixing bowl, combine grated zucchini with eggs, all-purpose flour, ground turmeric, ground black pepper, and shallot onion. Stir it well until you get the homogeneous mixture.

02 Preheat the skillet well and brush it with olive oil on the inside. Put 1 scoop of the zucchini mixture in hot oil and flatten it gently into the shape of the pancake.

03 Cook the pancake on medium heat for 4 minutes on each side. Repeat the same steps with the remaining zucchini mixture. Sprinkle the cooked zucchini pancakes with fresh dill.

Nutritional Value

Calories: 165	Fat: 10.8	Carbs: 12.6
Fiber: 2	Sugar: 1.3	Protein: 7.1

INGREDIENTS

- 2 cups zucchini, grated
- 3 eggs, beaten
- ¼ cup all-purpose flour
- 1 teaspoon ground black pepper
- ½ teaspoon ground turmeric
- 1 oz fresh dill, chopped
- 2 tablespoons olive oil
- 1 shallot onion, peeled, diced

13

INGREDIENTS

- 2 whole-grain bread slices
- 4 tablespoons cream cheese
- 2 figs, sliced
- 2 red Rubin basil leaves
- ¼ cup arugula, roughly chopped
- 1 teaspoon chia seeds
- 2 tablespoons apricot jam

Fig Toast

 🕐 10 mins 🍲 0 mins 👤 2

METHODS

01 Toast the bread slices in the toaster until they are light brown.

02 Let the bread slices cool, then spread the cream cheese on top. Top the bread slices with figs, arugula, and a sprinkle of chia seeds.

03 Serve the toast with apricot jam and basil leaves.

Nutritional Value

Calories: 246	Fat: 8.7	Carbs: 38.6
Fiber: 3.9	Sugar: 19.9	Protein: 5.3

INGREDIENTS

- ½ cup oatmeal
- 2 tablespoons chia seeds
- 1 cup blueberries
- 3 cups strawberries
- 1 cup Greek yogurt

Strawberries Smoothie Bowl

🕐 10 mins 🍲 0 mins 👤 2

METHODS

01 Slice 2 strawberries and set them aside. Put Greek yogurt, ¼ oatmeal, blueberries, and remaining strawberries into the blender. Blend the mixture until it is smooth.

02 Transfer the smooth mixture to the serving bowls. Top it with the slices of strawberries, remaining oatmeal, and sprinkle with the chia seeds.

Nutritional Value

Calories: 333	Fat: 8.6	Carbs: 50.9
Fiber: 13	Sugar: 22	Protein: 17.1

Breakfast Quiche

🕐 10 mins 🍲 75 mins 👤 4

INGREDIENTS

- 3 oz green onion, diced
- 4 oz Parmesan, grated
- 4 eggs, beaten
- 1 yellow onion, diced
- 1 tablespoon olive oil
- 4 oz coconut oil
- ½ cup all-purpose flour
- 2 eggs, boiled, peeled, chopped
- 1 teaspoon ground paprika

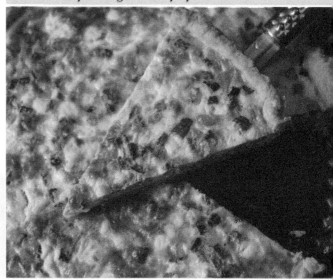

METHODS

01 Crust: combine all-purpose flour with coconut oil; knead the dough until it is smooth and soft; place it into a baking pan and flatten it to the shape of the pan.

02 Filling: preheat the skillet with olive oil; add onion and roast it for 3-5 minutes or until it is soft; combine the onion with paprika, Parmesan, green onion, and eggs, then stir everything.

03 Pour the mixture into the pie crust and spread it evenly. Cook the quiche at 350°F for 70 minutes.

Nutritional Value

Calories: 536   Fat: 44.8   Carbs: 17.9

Fiber: 1.8   Sugar: 2.3   Protein: 19.8

Breakfast Bowl

🕐 10 mins 🍲 15 mins 👤 2

INGREDIENTS

- 2 teaspoons chia seeds
- 2 cups cherry tomatoes, halved
- 1-pound chicken fillet
- 1 teaspoon olive oil
- 1 teaspoon ground black pepper
- 1 teaspoon dried basil
- 2 carrots, peeled, sliced
- 2 cups arugula
- 2 cups fresh spinach
- 2 eggs, boiled, peeled, halved
- 2 tablespoons lemon juice
- 2 tablespoons canola oil
- 2 red bell peppers, cut into strips

METHODS

01 Rub the chicken fillet with olive oil, dried basil, and ground black pepper. Grill the chicken in the preheated to 400°F grill for 7 minutes on each side. Slice the cooked chicken fillet.

02 Place the cherry tomatoes, carrots, eggs, and bell peppers into the serving bowls. Add arugula and spinach.

03 Place sliced chicken fillet on top. Sprinkle the meal with lemon juice, canola oil, and chia seeds.

Nutritional Value

Calories: 786   Fat: 40.8   Carbs: 28.2

Fiber: 9   Sugar: 14.9   Protein: 77.2

INGREDIENTS

- 4 oz plain granola
- ¼ cup chia seeds
- 1 cup blueberries
- ½ cup strawberries
- 1 ½ cups plain yogurt
- 1 tablespoon liquid honey
- A few mint leaves for garnish

Morning Chia Pudding

 10 mins   10 mins   2

METHODS

01   Mix chia seeds with 1 cup of plain yogurt and leave for 10 minutes in the fridge.

02   Leave out a few strawberries and blueberries for decoration. Blend the remaining yogurt, blueberries, and strawberries until smooth. Transfer the prepared yogurt with chia into the serving glass jars.

03   Top every glass jar with blended strawberry mixture and granola. Garnish the pudding with strawberries, blueberries, and mint leaves.

Nutritional Value

Calories: 589	Fat: 21.2	Carbs: 79
Fiber: 14.9	Sugar: 30.5	Protein: 21

INGREDIENTS

- 4 bananas, peeled, chopped
- ½ cup oatmeal flour
- ½ cup all-purpose flour
- 3 eggs, beaten
- 2 oz almonds, chopped
- ½ teaspoon ground turmeric
- ½ cup plain yogurt
- 1 teaspoon baking powder
- 1 teaspoon vanilla extract
- 1 tablespoon olive oil

Banana Crepes

 10 mins   10 mins   4

METHODS

01   Blend bananas in the food processor until you get a smooth texture. (Leave out one banana for decoration) Transfer this mixture to the mixing bowl. Add oatmeal flour, all-purpose flour, eggs, ground turmeric, plain yogurt, baking powder, and vanilla extract.

02   Carefully mix the ingredients until you get a homogeneous batter. Add olive oil and mix the batter again. Preheat the non-stick skillet well. Pour one ladle of the crepe batter into the skillet and flatten it in the shape of the crepe.

03   Cook the crepe on one side until the top is no longer we This typically takes around 1-2 minutes. Flip the crepe onto another side and cook it for additional 30 seconds. Repeat the same steps with the remaining crepe batter. Roll up the cooked crepes and garnish them with sliced bananas.

Nutritional Value

Calories: 378	Fat: 15.4	Carbs: 50.3
Fiber: 6.3	Sugar: 17.6	Protein: 13.2

SNACKS & APPETIZERS

INGREDIENTS

- 3-pounds ground beef
- 4 oz fresh parsley, chopped
- 3 oz fresh cilantro, chopped
- 1 tomato, chopped
- 1 tablespoon olive oil
- 1 lemon
- 1 teaspoon chili flakes
- 1 teaspoon salt
- 1 cup all-purpose flour
- 1 teaspoon instant yeast
- ¼ cup water
- 1 tablespoon canola oil

Ground Meat and Greens Cakes

 10 mins   25 mins   4

METHODS

O1 For the dough: in the mixing bowl, combine instant yeast with flour, water, and canola oil. Knead till the dough is smooth and non-sticky.

O2 Combine the remaining ingredients. Divide the dough into 4 even parts. Roll out each dough piece into the shape of a thin pizza circle.

O3 Top every dough circle with ground beef mixture. Bake the cakes for 25 minutes at 350°F.

Nutritional Value

Calories: 832	Fat: 29	Carbs: 28.8
Fiber: 3.2	Sugar: 1.3	Protein: 108.4

INGREDIENTS

- 3 medium zucchini, grated
- 4 eggs, beaten
- 2 tablespoons oatmeal
- 1 teaspoon ground black pepper
- 1 teaspoon baking powder
- ¼ cup canola oil

Zucchini Muffins

 10 mins   30 mins   4

METHODS

O1 Combine zucchini, eggs, and oatmeal to a homogeneous texture. Add all remaining ingredients and carefully mix.

O2 Pour the mixture into the muffin molds, filling each mold halfway. Bake the zucchini muffins for 30 minutes at 350°F.

Nutritional Value

Calories: 219	Fat: 18.5	Carbs: 7.9
Fiber: 2.1	Sugar: 2.9	Protein: 7.7

Tzaiziki

 10 mins   0 mins   3

INGREDIENTS

- 2 cups Greek yogurt
- 1 English cucumber, finely grated
- 1 tablespoon olive oil
- ¼ teaspoon garlic, grated
- 2 tablespoons lemon juice
- ½ cup fresh dill, chopped
- 1 teaspoon fresh mint, chopped

METHODS

O1 Place the grated cucumbers in the cheesecloth and gently squeeze out the excess water.

O2 Place the squeezed cucumbers in the bowl. Add all remaining ingredients and carefully combine everything. Store the cooked tzatziki in the fridge.

Nutritional Value

Calories: 179   Fat: 7.9   Carbs: 13.8

Fiber: 1.7   Sugar: 7.3   Protein: 5.8

Hummus

 10 mins   0 mins   3

INGREDIENTS

- 1 cup chickpeas, drained
- ¼ cup olive oil
- 1 garlic clove
- ¼ cup fresh cilantro
- 1 teaspoon chili flakes
- 1 teaspoon salt
- ½ lemon
- 1 teaspoon ground paprika

METHODS

O1 Put chickpeas in the food processor. Add olive oil, garlic, chili flakes, and salt.

O2 Add cilantro and blend the mixture until smooth. (leave out a little bit of cilantro for garnish)

O3 Transfer the mixture to the serving bowl and sprinkle with olive oil. Add the remaining cilantro, and ground paprika as a garnish.

Nutritional Value

Calories: 393   Fat: 21   Carbs: 42.1

Fiber: 12.2   Sugar: 7.5   Protein: 13.2

INGREDIENTS

- 1 ciabatta bread
- 1 cup Roma tomatoes, chopped
- 2 tablespoons olive oil
- ¼ cup fresh parsley, chopped
- 1/3 teaspoon salt

METHODS

01 Slice the ciabatta bread into the serving slices. Preheat the skillet well.

02 Put the ciabatta slices into the skillet and roast them for 1 minute on each side. Mix tomatoes with olive oil, parsley, and salt.

03 Top the cooked ciabatta slices with the tomato mixture.

Nutritional Value

Calories: 246   Fat: 11.2   Carbs: 35.3

Fiber: 2.6   Sugar: 3.6   Protein: 5.4

INGREDIENTS

- 1-pound mozzarella balls, sliced
- 1 tablespoon olive oil
- 1 oz fresh basil leaves
- 3 beefsteak tomatoes, sliced

Caprese

 10 mins 0 mins 5

METHODS

01 Place Mozzarella slices and tomatoes one by one on the serving plate.

02 Sprinkle the ingredients with the olive oil. Top everything with basil leaves.

Nutritional Value

Calories: 298   Fat: 22.4   Carbs: 3

Fiber: 1   Sugar: 2   Protein: 22.4

Bruschetta with Dried Tomatoes

🕐 10 mins   🍲 0 mins   👤 5

METHODS

O1   Spread the bread slices with ricotta cheese. Top with sun-dried tomatoes.

O2   Garnish the meal with mint leaves.

Nutritional Value

Calories: 69   Fat: 2.3   Carbs: 8.5

Fiber: 1.6   Sugar: 2.6   Protein: 4.5

INGREDIENTS

- 1 loaf of French bread, sliced
- ½ cup ricotta cheese
- 1-pound sun-dried tomatoes
- 1 oz fresh mint leaves

Tomato Ezme

🕐 10 mins   🍲 0 mins   👤 5

METHODS

O1   Put all ingredients in the food processor and blend until you get a smooth texture.

O2   Store the cooked ezme in the glass jar in the fridge.

Nutritional Value

Calories: 98   Fat: 8.7   Carbs: 5.7

Fiber: 1.4   Sugar: 3.3   Protein: 1.1

INGREDIENTS

- 2 cups beefsteak tomatoes, chopped
- 3 garlic cloves, peeled, chopped
- 1 teaspoon peppercorns
- 1 sweet pepper, chopped
- 3 tablespoons olive oil
- 1 chili pepper, chopped
- ½ teaspoon salt
- 2 tablespoons lemon juice

INGREDIENTS

- 1-pound nachos
- 1-pound ground beef
- 4 oz Parmesan, grated
- 1 sweet pepper, chopped
- 1 beefsteak tomato, chopped
- 1 oz green onion, chopped
- 1 tablespoon olive oil
- 1 tablespoon ground paprika

METHODS

O1   Put the nachos on the big serving plate. After this, preheat the skillet with olive oil. Add ground beef.

O2   Roast for 7 minutes or until the ground beef is cooked. Add ground paprika, tomato, onion, and sweet pepper. Stir the mixture and cook it for 10 more minutes.

O3   Top the nachos with ground beef mixture, then sprinkle with Parmesan.

Nutritional Value

Calories: 494	Fat: 25.3	Carbs: 23.6
Fiber: 4.6	Sugar: 2.1	Protein: 43.6

INGREDIENTS

- 1-pound chicken fillet, roughly chopped
- ½ teaspoon salt
- 1 teaspoon olive oil
- ½ teaspoon ground white pepper
- 1 eggplant, roughly chopped
- 1 zucchini, roughly chopped
- 2 cups cherry tomatoes

Antipasto Skewers

 10 mins 🍲 8 mins 👤 4

METHODS

O1   Put all ingredients in the mixing bowl and carefully combine. Then string all ingredients on the skewers one by one.

O2   Grill the antipasto at 400°F for 4 minutes on each side.

Nutritional Value

Calories: 279	Fat: 10.1	Carbs: 12
Fiber: 5.7	Sugar: 6.7	Protein: 35.3

SALAD RECIPES

INGREDIENTS

- 1-pound purple cabbage shredded
- 1 romaine lettuce, chopped
- 2 carrots, julienned
- 3 beefsteak tomatoes, chopped
- 2 tablespoons olive oil
- 1 tablespoon lemon juice
- ½ teaspoon dried basil

Summer Salad

 10 mins   0 mins   4

METHODS

O1   Dressing: mix lemon juice, olive oil, and dried basil.

O2   Put the purple cabbage, lettuce, carrot, and tomatoes into the salad bowl.

O3   Add dressing and carefully mix the salad.

Nutritional Value

Calories: 129	Fat: 7.5	Carbs: 15.3
Fiber: 4.9	Sugar: 4.8	Protein: 2.8

INGREDIENTS

- 1 teaspoon dried basil
- 4 oz Feta cheese, cubed
- 1 red onion, sliced
- 2 romaine lettuce, chopped
- 2 oz black olives, pitted
- 2 cups cherry tomatoes, halved
- 1 cup arugula, chopped
- 1 English cucumber, peeled, chopped
- 2 tablespoons olive oil
- ¼ teaspoon salt

Greek Salad

 10 mins   0 mins   4

METHODS

O1   In the salad bowl, place red onion, lettuce, black olives, cherry tomatoes, arugula, and cucumber. Sprinkle the salad with olive oil and salt, then gently mix.

O2   Place Feta cheese on top. Sprinkle the salad with dried basil.

Nutritional Value

Calories: 213	Fat: 15.2	Carbs: 15.9
Fiber: 3.6	Sugar: 7.7	Protein: 6.6

Light Caesar

 10 mins   20 mins   4

INGREDIENTS

- 2-pound chicken breast, skinless, boneless
- 1 tablespoon canola oil
- 1 tablespoon lemon juice
- 1 teaspoon ground black pepper
- 2 cups lettuce, chopped
- 3 oz fresh parsley, chopped
- 1 red onion, sliced
- 2 beefsteak tomatoes, roughly chopped

METHODS

01 Coat the chicken breast with lemon juice and ground black pepper, then grill at 375°F for 10 minutes on each side. Slice the chicken breast into servings.

02 In the serving bowl, mix lettuce with parsley, onion, tomatoes, and canola oil. Put the sliced chicken breast on the top of each serving.

Nutritional Value

Calories: 325   Fat: 9.6   Carbs: 7.6
Fiber: 2.4   Sugar: 3.3   Protein: 49.8

White Beans Salad

 5 mins   15 mins   4

INGREDIENTS

- 1-pound white beans, cooked, drained
- 2 beefsteak tomatoes, diced
- 1 red onion, peeled, chopped
- 1 oz green onion, diced
- 2 tablespoons olive oil
- 1 teaspoon ground black pepper
- 1 oz fresh dill, chopped

METHODS

01 In the mixing bowl, combine white beans with tomatoes, onion, green onion, olive oil, ground black pepper, and fresh dill.

02 Refrigerate the salad for 15 minutes.

Nutritional Value

Calories: 481   Fat: 8.5   Carbs: 78.1
Fiber: 19.9   Sugar: 5.4   Protein: 28.9

INGREDIENTS

- 1-pound chickpeas, cooked, drained
- 2 cups fresh baby spinach
- 1 English cucumber, sliced
- 1 red onion, diced
- 1 teaspoon ground black pepper
- 2 tablespoons olive oil

Spinach and Chickpea Salad

 10 mins ⬛ 0 mins 👤 4

METHODS

01 Put all ingredients in the mixing bowl and carefully incorporate.

02 Transfer the cooked salad into serving bowl.

Nutritional Value

Calories: 500 Fat: 14 Carbs: 75

Fiber: 21.2 Sugar: 14.6 Protein: 23.2

INGREDIENTS

- ½ cup quinoa, cooked
- 2 beefsteak tomatoes, sliced
- 1 English cucumber, chopped
- 3 oz fresh parsley, chopped
- 1 oz fresh arugula, chopped
- 1 carrot, peeled, julienned
- 1 teaspoon ground black pepper
- 2 tablespoons lemon juice
- 2 tablespoons olive oil
- ½ teaspoon black sesame seeds

Tabbouleh Salad

 10 mins ⬛ 0 mins 👤 4

METHODS

01 Put all ingredients in the mixing bowl and carefully combine.

02 Transfer the cooked salad onto the serving plates.

Nutritional Value

Calories: 186 Fat: 7.8 Carbs: 25.8

Fiber: 5.9 Sugar: 4.4 Protein: 4.7

Fine Bulgur Salad

🕐 10 mins   🍲 10 mins   👤 4

INGREDIENTS

- 1 cup fine bulgur wheat
- ½ cup hot water
- 1 romaine lettuce, chopped
- 1 beefsteak tomato, finely chopped
- 2 oz green onion, finely chopped
- 1 tablespoon tomato paste
- ¼ teaspoon salt
- 1 teaspoon ground black pepper
- 3 tablespoons olive oil
- 3 tablespoons lemon juice
- 1 oz pomegranate juice

METHODS

01 Mix bulgur with hot water and leave covered for 10 minutes. Add lettuce, tomato, green onion, tomato paste, salt, ground black pepper, olive oil, lemon juice, and pomegranate juice to the cooked bulgur.

02 Carefully mix the salad. Serve the salad cold.

Nutritional Value

Calories: 165   Fat: 10.9   Carbs: 15.7

Fiber: 3.5   Sugar: 3.6   Protein: 2.6

Red Cabbage and Pepper Salad

🕐 10 mins   🍲 0 mins   👤 4

INGREDIENTS

- 1 cup purple cabbage, shredded
- 1 cup white cabbage, shredded
- 1 green apple, peeled, julienned
- 1 sweet red pepper, julienned
- 1 tablespoon apple cider vinegar
- 2 tablespoons olive oil

METHODS

01 Put all ingredients in the mixing bowl and carefully combine.

Nutritional Value

Calories: 110   Fat: 7.2   Carbs: 12.6

Fiber: 2.7   Sugar: 8.6   Protein: 1

INGREDIENTS

- 1-pound radish, trimmed, sliced
- 3 oz fresh dill, chopped
- 4 mini cucumbers, cut into thin pieces
- ½ teaspoon salt
- 2 tablespoons olive oil

Spring Radish Salad

 10 mins   0 mins   4

METHODS

01   Put all ingredients in the mixing bowl and carefully combine.

02   Transfer the salad to the serving bowl.

Nutritional Value

Calories: 142	Fat: 8	Carbs: 17.7
Fiber: 4.7	Sugar: 2.1	Protein: 6

INGREDIENTS

- 4 small beets, cooked, sliced
- 1 tablespoon sunflower seeds
- 5 oz beetroot leaves, roughly chopped
- 4 oz Feta cheese, cubed
- 1 tablespoon olive oil

Beetroot Salad

 10 mins   0 mins   4

METHODS

01   Put the beets in the serving bowl. Add beet leaves and olive oil. Gently mix the ingredients, then top everything with Feta cheese.

02   Sprinkle the salad with sunflower seeds.

Nutritional Value

Calories: 161	Fat: 10.2	Carbs: 12.33
Fiber: 3	Sugar: 9.3	Protein: 7

Chopped Salad

🕐 10 mins   🍲 0 mins   👤 4

INGREDIENTS

- 2 English cucumbers, chopped
- 4 beefsteak tomatoes, chopped
- 3 oz green onion, chopped
- 3 oz fresh cilantro, chopped
- 1 lemon, sliced
- 2 tablespoons olive oil

METHODS

01 Put all ingredients in the mixing bowl and carefully combine.

02 Transfer the cooked salad to the serving bowl.

Nutritional Value

Calories: 121	Fat: 7.6	Carbs: 13.9
Fiber: 3.8	Sugar: 6.8	Protein: 3.1

Pasta Salad

🕐 10 mins   🍲 10 mins   👤 4

INGREDIENTS

- 6 oz pasta
- 1 cup broccoli, boiled, roughly chopped
- 1 cup cherry tomatoes, halved
- 1 teaspoon ground black pepper
- 1 tablespoon olive oil

METHODS

01 Cook pasta according to the directions of the manufacturer, then drain it and let it cool to room temperature.

02 Place the cooked pasta in the serving bowl. Add broccoli and cherry tomatoes.

03 Sprinkle the salad with olive oil and ground black pepper. Carefully stir the salad.

Nutritional Value

Calories: 170	Fat: 4.7	Carbs: 26.9
Fiber: 1.3	Sugar: 1.6	Protein: 5.9

INGREDIENTS

- 4 russet potatoes
- I yellow onion, sliced
- 4 cups water
- I cup Brussels sprouts, halved
- I tablespoon olive oil
- I teaspoon ground black pepper
- ¼ teaspoon salt
- I oz fresh mint, chopped

Poiaio Salad

 10 mins 🍲 20 mins 4

METHODS

O1 Peel and chop potatoes. Put them in the pot and add water. Add Brussels sprouts and boil the vegetables for 10 minutes or until they are soft.

O2 Preheat the skillet well and add olive oil. Add onion and roast it for 3 minutes. Drain the vegetables, then add them to the onion.

O3 Sprinkle the vegetables with ground black pepper and cook for additional 7 minutes. Stir them from time to time. Transfer everything to a serving bowl. Sprinkle the cooked salad with fresh mint.

Nutritional Value

Calories: 202	Fat: 3.9	Carbs: 39
Fiber: 7.2	Sugar: 4.1	Protein: 4.9

INGREDIENTS

- I tablespoon Dijon mustard
- 2 cups arugula, chopped
- I-pound chicken fillet
- I teaspoon ground black pepper
- I tablespoon olive oil
- 2 cups cherry tomatoes, chopped

Arugula and Chicken Salad

 10 mins 🍲 8 mins 4

METHODS

O1 Cover the chicken fillet in ground black pepper and olive oil and grill at 375°F for 4 minutes on each side.

O2 In the salad bowl, mix all the remaining ingredients. Chop the cooked chicken fillet and top the salad with it. Stir the salad gently.

Nutritional Value

Calories: 268	Fat: 12.3	Carbs: 4.4
Fiber: 1.5	Sugar: 2.6	Protein: 34.1

GRAINS, PASTA & RICE RECIPES

INGREDIENTS

- 1 oz fresh basil, chopped
- 1-pound penne pasta
- 1 cherry tomatoes
- ½ cup coconut cream
- 1 oz fresh cilantro, chopped
- 5 oz Parmigiana, grated

Parmigiana and Tomatoes Pasta

🕐 10 mins   🍲 35 mins   👤 4

METHODS

01   Cook penne pasta according to the directions of the manufacturer. Then place the cooked penne pasta in the baking pan.

02   Add tomatoes, coconut cream, Parmigiana, and cilantro. Mix the ingredients carefully and bake at 365°F for 25 minutes.

03   Sprinkle the cooked pasta with fresh basil.

Nutritional Value

Calories: 404	Fat: 9.9	Carbs: 65.4
Fiber: 1.3	Sugar: 1.9	Protein: 14.2

INGREDIENTS

- 1-pound spaghetti
- 1 cup tomatoes, crushed
- 1 teaspoon ground black pepper
- 1 teaspoon dried basil
- 1 teaspoon olive oil
- 5 oz extra lean ground beef
- ¼ teaspoon salt

Spaghetti Bolognese

🕐 10 mins   🍲 25 mins   👤 4

METHODS

01   Cook the spaghetti according to the directions of the manufacturer. Meanwhile, preheat the saucepan well.

02   Add olive oil and ground beef. Roast the ground beef for 5 minutes on medium heat. Stir it from time to time.

03   Add tomatoes, basil, and salt. Stir the ingredients well and cook for 5 minutes more.

04   Drain water from the spaghetti. Transfer the spaghetti to the beef sauce and carefully mix.

Nutritional Value

Calories: 407	Fat: 6.2	Carbs: 64.2
Fiber: 0.7	Sugar: 1.2	Protein: 22.6

Pesto and Zucchini Pasta

🕐 10 mins 🍲 25 mins 👤 4

METHODS

01 Cook the penne pasta according to the directions of the manufacturer. Preheat the coconut cream till it is hot and mix it with drained penne pasta.

02 Add pesto sauce and dried basil. Carefully mix the ingredients. Preheat the skillet well and add zucchini.

03 Roast the zucchini for 1 minute on each side. Add the cooked zucchini to the pasta. Gently stir the meal.

Nutritional Value

Calories: 554	Fat: 25.2	Carbs: 66.6
Fiber: 1.4	Sugar: 3.2	Protein: 16.7

INGREDIENTS

- 1-pound penne pasta
- 4 oz pesto sauce
- 1 zucchini, sliced
- 1 oz fresh basil, roughly chopped
- ¼ cup coconut cream
- 2 tablespoons olive oil

Seafood Spaghetti

🕐 10 mins 🍲 15 mins 👤 4

METHODS

01 Cook the spaghetti according to the directions of the manufacturer. Meanwhile, pour the olive oil into the saucepan.

02 Add chili flakes, dried oregano, thyme, mussels, and shrimp. Stir the ingredients carefully and cook for 5 minutes.

03 Add water and tomato paste. Cook the ingredients for an additional 5 minutes. Combine spaghetti with the seafood mixture.

Nutritional Value

Calories: 540	Fat: 7.5	Carbs: 68.9
Fiber: 0.8	Sugar: 3.9	Protein: 47.3

INGREDIENTS

- 1-pound spaghetti
- 3 tablespoons tomato paste
- 1 teaspoon chili flakes
- 1 teaspoon dried oregano
- 1 teaspoon fresh thyme
- 1/3 cup water
- 1 teaspoon olive oil
- 7 oz mussels in shells
- 1-pound shrimp, peeled

INGREDIENTS

- 1-pound fettuccine pasta
- 1 cup cremini mushrooms, sliced
- ½ cup coconut milk
- 1 teaspoon ground black pepper
- ¼ teaspoon salt
- ¼ cup fresh spinach, chopped
- 1 teaspoon olive oil

Creamy Mushrooms Fettuccine

🕐 10 mins   🍲 15 mins   👩 4

METHODS

01 Cook the fettuccine pasta according to the directions of the manufacturer. Meanwhile, preheat the saucepan well and pour olive oil inside.

02 Add mushrooms and salt and cook the ingredients for 4 minutes. Stir them well and add spinach. Cook the mixture for an additional 2 minutes.

03 Add coconut milk and ground black pepper. Close the lid and cook the mixture for 4 more minutes.

04 Drain the cooked pasta and add it to the mushroom mixture. Stir well, then cook on the low heat for 5 minutes more.

Nutritional Value

Calories: 503	Fat: 10.4	Carbs: 88.3
Fiber: 3	Sugar: 5.3	Protein: 15.2

INGREDIENTS

- 1-pound brown lentils
- 5 cups water
- ½ cup fresh cilantro, chopped
- 2 carrots, peeled, diced
- ¼ teaspoon ground nutmeg
- 1 yellow onion, peeled, diced
- 1 tablespoon olive oil
- ¼ cup coconut cream

Carrot and Lentils Bowl

🕐 10 mins   🍲 15 mins   👩 4

METHODS

01 Pour oil into the saucepan and preheat well. Add onion and cook it for 2 minutes. Throw in the carrot and stir the mixture well.

02 Add brown lentils, ground nutmeg, and water. Stir the ingredients gently and close the lid. Boil the meal for 10 minutes.

03 Then add coconut cream and cook the meal for 3 minutes more.

Nutritional Value

Calories: 203	Fat: 7.8	Carbs: 21.4
Fiber: 7.8	Sugar: 4.7	Protein: 8.5

Tender Bulgur with Tomatoes

🕐 10 mins | 🍲 25 mins | 👤 4

METHODS

01 Pour oil into the saucepan and preheat well. Add bulgur and roast it for 2 minutes.

02 Pour in the water and close the lid. Cook the bulgur for 7 minutes.

03 Add tomatoes and dill. Stir the bulgur and close the lid. Cook the meal for an additional 3 minutes.

04 Turn off the heat and let the meal sit for 10 minutes.

Nutritional Value

Calories: 377 | Fat: 9.2 | Carbs: 70.2
Fiber: 16.9 | Sugar: 1 | Protein: 14.5

INGREDIENTS

- 4 oz fresh dill, chopped
- 2 cups bulgur
- 4 cups water
- 1 beefsteak tomato, diced
- 2 tablespoons olive oil

Lemon and Herbs Couscous

🕐 10 mins | 🍲 15 mins | 👤 4

METHODS

01 Pour oil into the saucepan and preheat well. Add dried thyme and roast it for 1 minute.

02 Add couscous, lemon juice, lemon zest, corn kernels, and water. Stir well and bring the mixture to a boil.

03 Turn off the heat and close the lid. Let the meal rest for 10 minutes. Sprinkle the cooked meal with green sprouts.

Nutritional Value

Calories: 245 | Fat: 7.6 | Carbs: 38
Fiber: 3 | Sugar: 1 | Protein: 6.5

INGREDIENTS

- 1 cup couscous
- ½ cup corn kernels
- 1 cup hot water
- ¼ cup green sprouts
- 1 tablespoon lemon juice
- ½ teaspoon lemon zest, grated
- ½ teaspoon dried thyme
- 2 tablespoons olive oil

INGREDIENTS

- 2 cups oatmeal
- 1 cups coconut milk
- 1 cup raspberries
- 1 tablespoon Erythritol

Almond and Raspberries Oatmeal

 10 mins 🍲 10 mins 👤 4

METHODS

01 Bring the coconut milk to a boil, then add oatmeal.

02 Add Erythritol and stir gently. Cook on medium heat for 10 minutes, or until oatmeal has absorbed the coconut milk.

03 Transfer the cooked oatmeal to the serving bowls and top with raspberries.

Nutritional Value

Calories: 305 Fat: 17.1 Carbs: 33.8

Fiber: 6.2 Sugar: 4.2 Protein: 7

INGREDIENTS

- 4 sweet peppers
- 1 cup short-grain rice, boiled
- 4 oz extra-lean ground beef
- 1 tablespoon dried basil
- 6 oz mozzarella, shredded

Rice and Cheese Stuffed Peppers

 10 mins 55 mins 👤 4

METHODS

01 Cut the caps of the sweet peppers and remove the seeds. In the mixing bowl, combine rice with ground beef and basil.

02 Fill the sweet peppers with the rice mixture and top with Mozzarella. Cover the sweet peppers with pepper cups and bake at 350°F for 55 minutes.

Nutritional Value

Calories: 382 Fat: 10.3 Carbs: 47.5

Fiber: 2.2 Sugar: 6.1 Protein: 24.8

Beef Rice

🕐 10 mins   🍲 15 mins   👤 4

INGREDIENTS

- 1 cup long-grain rice
- 2 cups water
- 1 teaspoon ground turmeric
- ¼ teaspoon ground black pepper
- 1 carrot, peeled, grated
- 7 oz beef loin, chopped
- 2 tablespoons olive oil
- 1 garlic clove, peeled

METHODS

01 Preheat a saucepan with oil. Add beef and cook it for 2 minutes on each side.

02 Add garlic clove, grated carrot and cook the ingredients for 3 minutes more. Add rice, ground black pepper, and ground turmeric, then cover with water.

03 Stir the ingredients carefully, close the lid, and cook on medium heat for 10 minutes or until all liquid is evaporated.

Nutritional Value

Calories: 312   Fat: 10.9   Carbs: 39.8

Fiber: 1.1   Sugar: 1.4   Protein: 12.7

Rice in Wine Leaves

🕐 10 mins   🍲 20 mins   👤 4

INGREDIENTS

- 1 lemon, sliced
- 10 wine leaves
- 1 Roma tomato, diced
- 1 yellow onion, peeled, diced
- 1 teaspoon tomato paste
- 4 oz extra lean ground beef
- 1 teaspoon chili flakes
- 1 cup water

METHODS

01 In the mixing bowl, combine tomato with onion, ground beef, and chili flakes.

02 Place a small amount of the mixture on each wine leaf and roll them. Put the lemon slices in one layer at the bottom of the saucepan.

03 Add rolled wine leaves. Mix water with tomato paste and cover the rolls with it. Cover with the lid. Cook the meal on medium heat for 20 minutes.

Nutritional Value

Calories: 75   Fat: 2.1   Carbs: 6.4

Fiber: 1.6   Sugar: 3   Protein: 8.5

INGREDIENTS

- 7 oz smoked sausages, sliced
- 1 cup corn kernels
- ¼ cup sweet peas
- 1 carrot, diced
- 1 tablespoon olive oil
- 1 cup short-grain rice
- 2 cups water

Smoked Sausages and Vegeiable Rice

 10 mins   20 mins   4

METHODS

O1 Pour oil into the saucepan and preheat well. Add smoked sausages and roast them for 1 minute on each side.

O2 Add rice and stir until everything is combined. Add water, carrot, sweet peas, and corn kernels. Stir the ingredients gently and cover the saucepan with the lid.

O3 Cook the meal on medium heat for 15 minutes or until all liquid is evaporated.

Nutritional Value

Calories: 414	Fat: 18.4	Carbs: 47
Fiber: 2.5	Sugar: 2.6	Protein: 14.8

INGREDIENTS

- 1 oz fresh arugula
- 2 cups baby spinach, chopped
- 1 cup short-grain rice
- 1 cup coconut milk
- 1 ½ cup water
- 1 tablespoon olive oil
- ½ teaspoon ground black pepper
- 4 oz bacon, chopped
- 7 oz Parmesan, grated

Parmesan and Spinach Rice

 10 mins   25 mins   4

METHODS

O1 Pour oil into the saucepan and preheat well. Add bacon to the saucepan and cook it for 2 minutes, stirring occasionally.

O2 Add baby spinach and stir the ingredients well. Reduce the heat to low and continue cooking until the spinach reduces in size by approximately half.

O3 Add all remaining ingredients, stir well, then cover the saucepan with a lid. Cook the meal for 10 minutes. Let the cooked meal rest for an additional 10 minutes with a closed lid.

Nutritional Value

Calories: 496	Fat: 30.1	Carbs: 41.7
Fiber: 2.4	Sugar: 2.3	Protein: 15.8

FISH & SEAFOOD

INGREDIENTS

- 1 tablespoon olive oil
- 2 tablespoons lemon juice
- 1 teaspoon ground black pepper
- ¼ teaspoon salt
- 2-pounds salmon fillet

Broiled Salmon

 10 mins   10 mins   4

METHODS

O1   Rub the salmon fillet with lemon juice, olive oil, ground black pepper, and salt.

O2   Place it in the pan and broil for 5 minutes on each side on medium-high heat.

Nutritional Value

Calories: 333   Fat: 17.6   Carbs: 0.5

Fiber: 0.2   Sugar: 0.2   Protein: 44.1

INGREDIENTS

- 3 lemons, sliced
- 2 sea bream, trimmed, cleaned
- 1 cup fresh cilantro
- 1 garlic clove, peeled, chopped
- 2 tablespoons olive oil
- ¼ teaspoon ground nutmeg
- ¼ teaspoon ground coriander

Lemon Sea Bream

 10 mins   75 mins   4

METHODS

O1   Marinade: in the food processor, mix cilantro, garlic clove, olive oil, ground nutmeg, and ground coriander. Blend until smooth texture.

O2   Rub the seabream with the marinade well from inside and outside. Fill the fish with sliced lemon.

O3   Place the remaining lemon slices in the baking pan in one layer. Put the fish on top of the lemons and cover with aluminum foil. Bake the fish at 350°F for 75 minutes.

Nutritional Value

Calories: 371   Fat: 14.7   Carbs: 1

Fiber: 0.3   Sugar: 0.2   Protein: 54.6

Spiced Sea Bass with Cherry Tomatoes

🕐 10 mins   🍲 75 mins   👤 4

INGREDIENTS

- 1 oz fresh sage
- 1 oz fresh dill
- 1 cup cherry tomatoes
- 1 lemon, sliced
- 1 teaspoon olive oil
- ½ teaspoon ground black pepper
- ½ teaspoon ground coriander
- 2 sea bass, trimmed, cleaned

METHODS

01 Rub the sea bass with olive oil, ground black pepper, and ground coriander.

02 Put a few lemon slices, half of the dill, and sage inside the fish. Transfer the fish to the baking pan.

03 Add cherry tomatoes, remaining dill, and sage. Cover the baking pan with aluminum foil and bake at 355°F for 75 minutes.

Nutritional Value

Calories: 315	Fat: 10	Carbs: 13.9
Fiber: 4.4	Sugar: 1.3	Protein: 2.6

Pesto Sea Bass

🕐 10 mins   🍲 60 mins   👤 4

INGREDIENTS

- 1 cup arugula, chopped
- 1 cup lettuce, chopped
- 1 lemon
- ½ cup radish, sliced
- ½ cup cherry tomatoes, sliced
- ½ cup pesto sauce
- 1 teaspoon ground black pepper
- 4 sea bass fillets
- 1 tablespoon olive oil

METHODS

01 Rub the sea bass fillet with ground black pepper and pesto sauce (leave 2 tablespoons of pesto sauce for serving). Transfer the fish to the baking tray and cook at 360°F for 60 minutes.

02 Garnish: mix arugula with lettuce, radish, and cherry tomatoes. Cut the lemon into halves and squeeze one-half of the lemon over the greens mixture.

03 Sprinkle the mixture with olive oil and carefully stir. Place the cooked seabass on the plate and sprinkle with juice from the remaining lemon half. Add garnish.

Nutritional Value

Calories: 415	Fat: 30.8	Carbs: 5.7
Fiber: 2.6	Sugar: 4.2	Protein: 29.8

INGREDIENTS

- 2 mackerel, trimmed, cleaned
- 1 tablespoon dried thyme
- 1 tablespoon lemon juice
- ½ teaspoon olive oil

Thyme Mackerel

 10 mins   10 mins   4

METHODS

O1   Cut the mackerel into 4 fillets. Rub the fish fillets with olive oil, lemon juice, and dried thyme.

O2   Grill the fish for 5 minutes per side at 375°F.

Nutritional Value

Calories: 123	Fat: 8.5	Carbs: 0.5
Fiber: 0.3	Sugar: 0.1	Protein: 10.6

INGREDIENTS

- 2-pounds mussels, rinsed
- 1/3 teaspoon ground black pepper
- 5 oz Parmesan, grated
- 1 teaspoon olive oil
- 1 tablespoon water
- ½ teaspoon garlic, minced
- 4 cups water, for boiling

Tender Mussel Shells

 10 mins   20 mins   4

METHODS

O1   Place the mussels in a pan and add water. Bring the water to a boil and cook the mussels for 7 minutes.

O2   Remove the mussels from the water and detach the top shell from each mussel, leaving them attached to the bottom shells. Mix ground black pepper, water, Parmesan, and garlic.

O3   Coat mussels with garlic mixture. Transfer the mussels to the baking tray and bake at 365°F for 10 minutes.

Nutritional Value

Calories: 320	Fat: 13.9	Carbs: 9.9
Fiber: 0.1	Sugar: 0	Protein: 38.4

Tender Mackerel Cooked in Foil

🕐 10 mins 🍲 80 mins 👤 4

METHODS

O1 Rub the mackerel fillets with ground black pepper and olive oil.

O2 Place the mackerel fillets on a sheet of aluminum foil. Top the fillets with lemon, cilantro, and tomatoes.

O3 Wrap the foil and transfer it to the oven. Cook the meal at 365°F for 80 minutes.

Nutritional Value

Calories: 627   Fat: 42.3   Carbs: 4.2

Fiber: 1.4   Sugar: 2   Protein: 54.9

INGREDIENTS

- 2-pounds mackerel fillet
- 1 lemon, sliced
- 2 tomatoes, roughly chopped
- 1 cup fresh cilantro, roughly chopped
- 1 teaspoon ground black pepper
- ½ tablespoon olive oil

Grilled Trout Stuffed with Vegetables

🕐 10 mins 🍲 30 mins 👤 4

METHODS

O1 Rub the trout with ground black pepper, ground nutmeg, lemon juice, and olive oil. Transfer the fish to the grill. Grill it for 10 minutes on each side at 375°F.

O2 Place the sweet peppers, zucchini, eggplant, and cherry tomatoes on the grill and cook them for 2 minutes on each side at 375°F.

O3 Place all grilled ingredients on the serving plate.

Nutritional Value

Calories: 524   Fat: 23.4   Carbs: 36.8

Fiber: 5.9   Sugar: 8   Protein: 63

INGREDIENTS

- 2 sweet peppers, roughly chopped
- 1 zucchini, sliced
- 1 eggplant, sliced
- ½ cup cherry tomatoes
- 2-pound trout, trimmed, cleaned
- 1 teaspoon ground black pepper
- ½ teaspoon ground nutmeg
- 1 tablespoon olive oil
- 1 tablespoon lemon juice

INGREDIENTS

- 2-pounds anchovies, trimmed, cleaned
- 2 tablespoons olive oil
- 1 lemon
- 1 cup fresh dill
- ½ yellow onion, sliced
- ½ cup fresh parsley

Lemony Anchovies

 10 mins 10 mins 👩 4

METHODS

O1　Pour olive oil into the skillet. Place the anchovies in the skillet in one layer. Cover the skillet with the lid and cook anchovies for 5 minutes on each side.

O2　Transfer the cooked anchovies to the serving plate and garnish them with sliced lemon, onion, dill, and parsley.

Nutritional Value

Calories: 579	Fat: 29.7	Carbs: 9.8
Fiber: 2.6	Sugar: 1	Protein: 68.5

INGREDIENTS

- 2-pounds sardines, trimmed, cleaned
- 2 tablespoons olive oil
- 1 lemon

Lemony Sardines

 10 mins  10 mins 👩 4

METHODS

O1　Pour olive oil into the skillet. Preheat the olive oil well, then add sardines. Roast the sardines for 4 minutes on each side.

O2　Transfer the cooked sardines to the serving plate and drizzle with squeezed lemon juice.

Nutritional Value

Calories: 536	Fat: 33	Carbs: 1.4
Fiber: 0.4	Sugar: 0.4	Protein: 56

Lemongrass Lobster

🕐 10 mins   🍲 30 mins   👤 4

METHODS

01   In the mixing bowl, combine cream cheese with dried lemongrass, parmesan, and ground black pepper.

02   Stuff the lobster halves with the cream cheese mixture and bake for 30 minutes at 355°F.

03   Garnish the meal with cherry tomatoes, lemon, and broccoli.

Nutritional Value

Calories: 229   Fat: 15.2   Carbs: 6.6

Fiber: 1.7   Sugar: 2   Protein: 18.4

INGREDIENTS

- 2 lobsters, halved
- ½ cup cream cheese
- 1 teaspoon dried lemongrass
- 3 oz Parmesan, grated
- 1 teaspoon ground black pepper
- 1 cup cherry tomatoes
- 1 lemon, roughly chopped
- 1 cup broccoli, boiled

Thyme and Rosemary Shrimp

🕐 10 mins   🍲 5 mins   👤 4

METHODS

01   Combine the shrimp with olive oil, dried thyme, and dried rosemary.

02   Preheat the skillet well. Place the shrimp in the skillet and cook them for 2 minutes per side.

Nutritional Value

Calories: 301   Fat: 74   Carbs: 3.8

Fiber: 0.2   Sugar: 0   Protein: 51.7

INGREDIENTS

- 2-pounds shrimp, peeled
- 1 tablespoon olive oil
- 1 teaspoon dried thyme
- 1 teaspoon dried rosemary

INGREDIENTS

- 2-pounds shrimp, peeled
- 2 tablespoons piri piri sauce
- 4 tablespoons olive oil
- 2 garlic cloves, peeled, chopped
- ¼ cup fresh parsley, chopped
- 1 red chili pepper

Piri Piri Shrimp

 10 mins 10 mins 👩 4

METHODS

01 Preheat the olive oil in the skillet and add shrimp. Roast them for 2 minutes. Then stir the shrimp well, add piri piri, chili pepper, and garlic, then cover with the lid.

02 Cook the shrimp on medium-low heat for 5 minutes more. Sprinkle the cooked shrimp with parsley.

Nutritional Value

Calories: 394	Fat: 17.9	Carbs: 4.3
Fiber: 0.2	Sugar: 0.1	Protein: 51.9

INGREDIENTS

- 2-pounds shrimp, peeled
- 4 garlic cloves, sliced
- ½ cup fresh dill, chopped
- 2 tablespoons olive oil

Garlic and Dill Shrimps

 10 mins 10 mins 👩 4

METHODS

01 Preheat olive oil in the skillet. Add garlic and roast it for 1 minute.

02 Add shrimp and cook them for 2 minutes per side. Throw in dill, stir the meal carefully, and cook it for an additional 1 minute.

Nutritional Value

Calories: 310	Fat: 15.3	Carbs: 29.8
Fiber: 2.4	Sugar: 16.5	Protein: 14.9

POULTRY RECIPES

INGREDIENTS

- 2 Cornish hen
- 1-pound small russet potatoes
- 1 orange, sliced
- 1 oz fresh rosemary
- 1 teaspoon ground black pepper
- 3 tablespoons olive oil
- ½ teaspoon ground coriander
- ½ teaspoon ground paprika
- ½ teaspoon ground turmeric

Whole Cornish Hens with Oranges

🕐 10 mins 🍲 85 mins   6

METHODS

O1 Rub the Cornish hens with coriander, paprika, and turmeric. Drizzle the potatoes with olive oil.

O2 Transfer the hens and potatoes to the baking tray. Add rosemary and oranges. Bake the Cornish hens at 355°F for 85 minutes.

Nutritional Value

Calories: 215	Fat: 9.3	Carbs: 23.3
Fiber: 4.7	Sugar: 3.7	Protein: 11.1

INGREDIENTS

- 2-pounds chicken drumsticks
- 2 garlic cloves, minced
- 3 tablespoons olive oil
- ½ cup cherry tomatoes, crushed
- 1 teaspoon peppercorns
- 1 teaspoon dried basil
- 3 tablespoons lemon juice
- ½ teaspoon salt

Basil Chicken Drumsticks

🕐 10 mins 🍲 55 mins   4

METHODS

O1 Mix cherry tomatoes, minced garlic with olive oil, peppercorns, dried basil, salt, and lemon juice.

O2 Then put the chicken drumsticks in the tomato mixture and leave for 10 minutes to marinate.

O3 Transfer the chicken drumsticks and all remaining tomato mixture to the baking tray and bake at 375°F for 55 minutes.

Nutritional Value

Calories: 484	Fat: 23.6	Carbs: 2
Fiber: 0.5	Sugar: 0.9	Protein: 62.8

Turkey and Mushrooms Sausages

🕐 10 mins 🍲 65 mins 👩 4

METHODS

01 In the mixing bowl, combine mushrooms with dried thyme, ground black pepper, minced turkey, and onion. Fill the sausage cases with turkey mixture.

02 Pour olive oil into the skillet, then place the sausages inside. Bake the sausages at 386°F for 65 minutes.

Nutritional Value

Calories: 215   Fat: 9.3   Carbs: 23.3

Fiber: 4.7   Sugar: 3.7   Protein: 11.1

INGREDIENTS

- 4 sausage case
- 1 cup cremini mushrooms, diced
- 1-pound turkey fillet, minced
- 1 teaspoon dried thyme
- 1 tablespoon olive oil
- 1 teaspoon ground black pepper
- 1 yellow onion, peeled, minced

Onion Chicken Thighs

🕐 15 mins 🍲 60 mins 👩 4

METHODS

01 In the mixing bowl, combine onion, Herbs de Provence, and olive oil. Grate the zest from the lemon and squeeze juice. Add the lemon zest and juice to the onion mixture.

02 Coat chicken tights with onion mixture and leave for 10 minutes to marinate. Transfer the marinated chicken to the baking tray and bake at 375°F for 60 minutes.

Nutritional Value

Calories: 436   Fat: 7.5   Carbs: 6.5

Fiber: 1.6   Sugar: 2.7   Protein: 38.8

INGREDIENTS

- 8 chicken tights, boneless
- 2 yellow onions, minced
- 1 tablespoon Herbs de Provence
- 3 tablespoons olive oil
- 1 lemon

INGREDIENTS

- 1 cup tomatoes, crushed
- 1 teaspoon mustard seeds
- 1 tablespoon ground paprika
- ¼ cup wine vinegar
- ½ teaspoon ground black pepper
- 1 tablespoon dried basil
- 2 tablespoons olive oil
- 2-pounds chicken wings

Chicken Wings in Tomato Sauce

 20 mins   60 mins   4

METHODS

O1   Put tomatoes, mustard seeds, ground paprika, wine vinegar, ground black pepper, dried basil, and olive oil in the food processor. Blend the mixture until smooth.

O2   Coat the chicken wings with tomato mixture and let it marinate for 15-20 minutes.

O3   Transfer the chicken wings and all remaining tomato sauce to the baking tray and bake it for 60 minutes at 375°F.

Nutritional Value

Calories: 509	Fat: 24.4	Carbs: 4.4
Fiber: 1.5	Sugar: 1.5	Protein: 66.5

INGREDIENTS

- 2-pounds chicken drumsticks
- 1 yellow onion, peeled, diced
- 2 sweet peppers, chopped
- 2 tablespoons Dijon mustard
- ¼ cup coconut milk
- 1 teaspoon ground black pepper
- 1 tablespoon olive oil
- ½ cup tomatoes, chopped

Mustard Chicken Drumsticks

 10 mins   50 mins   4

METHODS

O1   In the mixing bowl, combine mustard with the onion, coconut milk, ground black pepper, and tomatoes.

O2   Pour the olive oil into the cast iron skillet and preheat well. Add the chicken drumsticks and roast them for 3 minutes on each side.

O3   Add the mustard mixture and carefully mix. Transfer the skillet to the oven and cook at 375°F for 40 minutes.

Nutritional Value

Calories: 488	Fat: 20.6	Carbs: 9.5
Fiber: 2.4	Sugar: 5.3	Protein: 64.2

Chicken Cutlets with Arugula and Tomatoes

 10 mins 🍲 10 mins 👤 4

METHODS

01 Slice the chicken fillets into cutlets and rub them with ground black pepper and ground cumin.

02 Pour the olive oil into the skillet, preheat well, then place the chicken cutlets inside. Roast them for 5 minutes per side on medium heat.

03 Mix arugula with cherry tomatoes and lemon juice. Transfer the cooked chicken cutlets to the serving plate and garnish them with arugula mixture.

Nutritional Value

Calories: 243	Fat: 11.5	Carbs: 2.6
Fiber: 0.9	Sugar: 1.5	Protein: 31.2

INGREDIENTS

- 3 chicken fillets
- 1 teaspoon ground black pepper
- 1 tablespoon olive oil
- ¼ teaspoon ground cumin
- 2 cups arugula, roughly chopped
- 1 cup cherry tomatoes, halved
- 1 tablespoon lemon juice

Chicken Patties with Tomato Sauce

 10 mins 🍲 10 mins 👤 4

METHODS

01 Put the chicken fillet in the mixing bowl. Add green onion, basil, egg, and yellow onion. Combine the mixture well. Preheat the non-stick skillet well. Make the small patties from the chicken mixture and place the patties in the hot skillet.

02 Cook the patties for 4 minutes per side on medium-low heat. The tomato sauce: put tomatoes, garlic, ground black pepper, cayenne pepper, and olive oil in the food processor and blend until smooth.

03 Transfer the tomato mixture to the saucepan and bring to a boil. Let the sauce cool down. Place the cooked chicken patties on the serving plate and garnish them with tomato sauce.

Nutritional Value

Calories: 266	Fat: 10.9	Carbs: 5.7
Fiber: 1.5	Sugar: 2.6	Protein: 35.2

INGREDIENTS

- 1-pound chicken fillet, minced
- 1 oz green onion, diced
- 1 tablespoon dried basil
- 1 egg, beaten
- 1 yellow onion, minced
- 1 garlic clove
- 1 cup Roma tomatoes, chopped
- 1 teaspoon olive oil
- 1 teaspoon ground black pepper
- ½ teaspoon cayenne pepper

INGREDIENTS

- 2-pounds chicken wings
- 1 teaspoon dried thyme
- 1 teaspoon dried rosemary
- 1 garlic bulb, peeled
- ½ cup cherry tomatoes
- 1 tablespoon olive oil
- ½ teaspoon ground paprika

Roasted Rosemary Chicken Wings

 10 mins 60 mins 4

METHODS

01 Place the chicken wings on the baking tray. Sprinkle the chicken with dried thyme, rosemary, paprika, and olive oil.

02 Add garlic and cherry tomatoes. Bake the meal at 365°F for 60 minutes.

Nutritional Value

Calories: 471   Fat: 20.5   Carbs: 2.1

Fiber: 0.6   Sugar: 0.6   Protein: 65.9

INGREDIENTS

- 2-pounds chicken fillet, roughly chopped
- 1 teaspoon minced garlic
- 1 tablespoon olive oil
- 1 teaspoon dried rosemary

Garlic Chicken Bites

 10 mins   10 mins 4

METHODS

01 Mix the chopped chicken with minced garlic, olive oil, and rosemary.

02 Preheat the grill to 400°F. Place the chicken on the grill and cook it for 4 minutes on each side.

Nutritional Value

Calories: 463   Fat: 20.4   Carbs: 0.4

Fiber: 0.1   Sugar: 0   Protein: 65.7

MEAT
RECIPES

INGREDIENTS

- 3 carrots, peeled, roughly chopped
- 1 bay leaf
- 1-pound beef loin, roughly chopped
- 1 yellow onion, roughly chopped
- 1 Russet potato, roughly chopped
- 2 cups water
- 1 teaspoon salt
- 1 teaspoon peppercorns
- 1 cup tomatoes, chopped
- ½ teaspoon caraway seeds
- 1 teaspoon olive oil

Beef Goulash

 10 mins 40 mins 6

METHODS

O1 Pour the olive oil into the pan and preheat. Add chopped onion and roast for 3 minutes. Add beef loin and roast the ingredients for 2 minutes more.

O2 Add carrot and potatoes, stir well, and cook the ingredients for 3 minutes more. Add salt, peppercorns, bay leaf, caraway seeds, and tomatoes.

O3 Add water and stir the mixture gently. Cover the pan with the lid and cook the meal for 30 minutes on medium-high heat.

Nutritional Value

Calories: 212	Fat: 7.2	Carbs: 15.2
Fiber: 2.4	Sugar: 2.8	Protein: 22.1

INGREDIENTS

- 1 cup Roma tomatoes, crushed
- 1 onion, minced
- 1 garlic clove, minced
- 1 egg, beaten
- 3 oz fresh dill, chopped
- 1 oz fresh basil, chopped
- 2-pounds beef loin, minced
- 1 tablespoon olive oil

Basil and Tomato Meatballs

 15 mins 30 mins 4

METHODS

O1 In the mixing bowl, combine the onion with garlic, egg, dill, basil, and beef loin. When the mixture is homogeneous, make the meatballs from it.

O2 Pour olive oil into the skillet and preheat well. Add the meatballs and roast them for 3 minutes on each side.

O3 Cover the meatballs with crushed tomatoes. Transfer the skillet with meatballs to the oven and bake them at 375°F for 20 minutes.

Nutritional Value

Calories: 534	Fat: 24.6	Carbs: 16.7
Fiber: 4.2	Sugar: 2.5	Protein: 67.3

Peppercorns Beef Steaks

 10 mins 12 mins 👨 4

METHODS

01 Drizzle the beef steaks with olive oil and sprinkle with peppercorns, dried basil, ground cumin, and chili flakes.

02 Preheat the grill to 390°F. Place the beef steaks inside the grill and cook for 6 minutes on each side.

Nutritional Value

Calories: 173 Fat: 6.6 Carbs: 1.4

Fiber: 0.1 Sugar: 0 Protein: 26

INGREDIENTS

- 4 beef steaks
- 1 tablespoon peppercorns, crushed
- 1 teaspoon dried basil
- ¼ teaspoon ground cumin
- ¼ teaspoon chili flakes
- 1 teaspoon olive oil

Garlic Lamb on Rack

 15 mins 80 mins 👩 4

METHODS

01 To the blender, put garlic cloves, spinach, and ground black pepper. Blend the mixture until smooth.

02 Rub the lamb on the rack with the garlic mixture. Let the meat marinate for 15 minutes.

03 Wrap the meat in aluminum foil and bake at 385°F for 80 minutes.

Nutritional Value

Calories: 477 Fat: 30.6 Carbs: 1.1

Fiber: 0.3 Sugar: 0.1 Protein: 46.5

INGREDIENTS

- 1-pound chicken fillet, minced
- 1 oz green onion, diced
- 1 tablespoon dried basil
- 1 egg, beaten
- 1 yellow onion, minced
- 1 garlic clove
- 1 cup Roma tomatoes, chopped
- 1 teaspoon olive oil
- 1 teaspoon ground black pepper
- ½ teaspoon cayenne pepper

INGREDIENTS

- 2-pounds beef loin, chopped
- 5 bay leaves
- 2 yellow onions, sliced
- 2 tablespoons olive oil
- 1 teaspoon peppercorns
- 3 cups water

Bay Leaf and Onion Beef Bites

 15 mins   40 mins   4

METHODS

01   Pour olive oil into the pan and add onion. Roast the onion for 3 minutes. Stir it well, add peppercorns, bay leaf, water, and beef loin.

02   Cover the pan with the lid and cook the meal on medium-high heat for 40 minutes.

Nutritional Value

Calories: 421	Fat: 23.3	Carbs: 8.2
Fiber: 1.3	Sugar: 5	Protein: 42.5

INGREDIENTS

- 1-pound bacon, sliced
- 1 teaspoon Erythritol
- 1 tablespoon olive oil
- 1 tablespoon lemon juice
- 1 teaspoon ground black pepper

Sweet and Sour Bacon

 15 mins   5 mins   4

METHODS

01   In the mixing bowl, combine lemon juice, olive oil, Erythritol, and ground black pepper.

02   Brush the bacon with the sour-sweet mixture and transfer to the preheated skillet. Roast the bacon for 2 minutes on each side.

Nutritional Value

Calories: 646	Fat: 50.9	Carbs: 2
Fiber: 0.2	Sugar: 0.1	Protein: 42.1

Lasagna

🕐 15 mins   🍲 35 mins   👩 4

METHODS

01 Pour olive oil into the skillet. Add onion and roast it for 2 minutes. Throw in ground beef and roast it for 7 more minutes. Add crushed tomatoes, carefully stir the mixture and cook for 1 minute more.

02 Place 2 lasagna pasta in the baking tray. Put 4 tablespoons of ground beef mixture over the lasagna pasta, flatten it, then cover with some Mozzarella cheese. Cover it with 2 more lasagna pasta.

03 Repeat the same steps till you use all ingredients. Bake lasagna at 375°F for 25 minutes.

Nutritional Value

Calories: 515   Fat: 18.8   Carbs: 56

Fiber: 8.7   Sugar: 18.1   Protein: 28.4

INGREDIENTS

- 1 cup Mozzarella, shredded
- 1 cup crushed tomatoes
- 1 cup extra-lean ground beef
- 1 teaspoon salt
- 6 lasagna pasta, boiled
- 1 teaspoon olive oil
- 1 yellow onion, peeled, diced

Turkish Pide

🕐 15 mins   🍲 30 mins   👦 4

METHODS

01 In the mixing bowl, combine flour with nutritional yeast, and water. Stir the mixture gently, add olive oil, and knead the dough.

02 Roll out the dough into the shape of an oval pizza. Mix beef with sweet pepper, thyme, salt, and tomato.

03 Spread the beef mixture over the dough and bake it at 365°F for 30 minutes.

Nutritional Value

Calories: 350   Fat: 11.1   Carbs: 27.9

Fiber: 1.8   Sugar: 2.3   Protein: 34.5

INGREDIENTS

- 1-pound beef loin, diced
- 1 sweet pepper, diced
- 1 beefsteak tomato, chopped
- 1 teaspoon dried thyme
- ½ teaspoon salt
- 1 cup all-purpose flour
- 1 teaspoon nutritional yeast
- ¼ cup water
- 1 teaspoon olive oil

INGREDIENTS

- 1-pound ground pork
- 1 teaspoon dried rosemary
- 2 eggs, beaten
- 1 teaspoon minced garlic
- ¼ teaspoon ground black pepper

Rosemary Meatloaf

 15 mins 50 mins 4

METHODS

01 Mix all ingredients in the mixing bowl. Transfer the meat mixture to the loaf mold and flatten it well.

02 Bake the meatloaf for 50 minutes at 385°F.

Nutritional Value

Calories: 196	Fat: 6.2	Carbs: 0.7
Fiber: 0.2	Sugar: 0.2	Protein: 32.5

INGREDIENTS

- 1-pound extra lean ground pork
- ½ cup Mozzarella cheese, shredded
- 1 egg, beaten
- ¼ teaspoon ground cumin
- 1 teaspoon dried garlic

Cheese and Pork Balls

 15 mins 30 mins 4

METHODS

01 Mix ground pork with cheese, egg, ground cumin, and dried garlic.

02 Form the balls from the mixture and place them on the baking tray. Bake the pork balls for 30 minutes at 365°F.

Nutritional Value

Calories: 189	Fat: 5.7	Carbs: 0.5
Fiber: 0	Sugar: 0.1	Protein: 32.1

VEGETABLE RECIPES

INGREDIENTS

- 1-pound zucchini flowers
- 1 cup ricotta cheese
- 1 cup spinach, chopped
- 1 cup fresh parsley, chopped
- 2 tablespoons olive oil
- 2 eggs, beaten

Stuffed Zucchini Flowers

 15 mins 🍲 10 mins 👧 4

METHODS

O1 Put the ricotta cheese, spinach, and parsley in the blender. Blend the mixture until smooth. Fill each zucchini flower with a ricotta cheese mixture.

O2 Preheat olive oil in the skillet. Dip every zucchini flower into the beaten egg.

O3 Transfer the dipped zucchini flowers to the hot oil and roast them for 1 minute on each side or until the zucchini flowers are golden brown.

Nutritional Value

Calories: 184	Fat: 14.2	Carbs: 4.6
Fiber: 0.7	Sugar: 0.5	Protein: 10.5

INGREDIENTS

- 3 eggplants, sliced
- 2 sweet peppers, roughly chopped
- ½ cup green olives, pitted
- 1 tablespoons capers
- 1 tablespoon fresh basil, chopped
- 1 tablespoon olive oil
- ½ cup water

Eggplant Ragout

 15 mins 🍲 30 mins 👦 4

METHODS

O1 Pour olive oil into the pan and preheat it. Throw in eggplants and roast them for 2 minutes per side. Transfer the roasted eggplants to the baking pan.

O2 Add sweet peppers, green olives, capers, basil, and water. Cover the pan with the lid and saute the ragout for 25 minutes on medium-high heat.

Nutritional Value

Calories: 158	Fat: 4.9	Carbs: 29.2
Fiber: 15.6	Sugar: 15.3	Protein: 4.8

Fragrant Grilled Tomatoes

 10 mins   5 mins 4

INGREDIENTS

- 1-pound cherry tomatoes, halved
- 1 teaspoon olive oil
- 1 teaspoon dried thyme

METHODS

01 Drizzle the cherry tomatoes with olive oil and sprinkle with dried thyme.

02 Preheat the grill to 380°F. Place the cherry tomatoes on the grill and cook them for 2 minutes.

Nutritional Value

Calories: 31	Fat: 1.4	Carbs: 4.6
Fiber: 1.5	Sugar: 3	Protein: 1

Vegetable Gratin

 15 mins   40 mins 4

INGREDIENTS

- 4 beefsteak tomatoes, sliced
- 2 eggplants, sliced
- 1 cup Mozzarella, shredded
- ½ teaspoon ground cumin
- 1 teaspoon fresh basil, chopped
- 1 teaspoon olive oil

METHODS

01 Brush the baking pan with olive oil. Put the tomatoes and eggplants in the baking pan one by one. Cover with Mozzarella cheese.

02 Sprinkle the gratin with ground cumin and basil. Bake the meal at 365°F for 40 minutes.

Nutritional Value

Calories: 122	Fat: 3.2	Carbs: 21.3
Fiber: 11.2	Sugar: 11.5	Protein: 5.8

INGREDIENTS

- 2-pounds Brussels sprouts halved
- 1 teaspoon ground black pepper
- 2 tablespoons olive oil

METHODS

O1 Sprinkle the Brussels sprouts with ground black pepper and olive oil.

O2 Then place the vegetables on the baking tray and flatten them well. Bake the vegetables at 350°F for 35 minutes.

Nutritional Value

Calories: 143	Fat: 8.2	Carbs: 16.4
Fiber: 6	Sugar: 4	Protein: 5.8

INGREDIENTS

- 1 cup ricotta cheese
- 1 zucchini, sliced
- ½ cup corn kernels, boiled
- 1 teaspoon ground black pepper
- 1/3 cup water
- 1 cup all-purpose flour
- 2 tablespoons olive oil

Zucchini and Corn Pie

🕐 15 mins 🍲 30 mins 👤 4

METHODS

O1 In the mixing bowl, combine all-purpose flour and water. Add olive oil and knead the dough until it reaches a non-sticky consistency.

O2 Roll out the dough in the shape of a square and spread it over with ricotta cheese.

O3 Top the ricotta cheese with the sliced zucchini, corn kernels, and ground black pepper. Bake the pie at 375°F for 30 minutes.

Nutritional Value

Calories: 285	Fat: 12.6	Carbs: 32.7
Fiber: 2.1	Sugar: 1.8	Protein: 11.6

Zucchini Sticks

🕐 15 mins   🍲 20 mins   👤 4

METHODS

O1   Sprinkle the zucchini sticks with olive oil, peppercorns, dried basil, and chili flakes.

O2   Place the zucchini sticks in one layer on a parchment-lined baking tray. Bake the zucchini stick for 20 minutes at 350°F.

Nutritional Value

Calories: 47	Fat: 3.7	Carbs: 3.6
Fiber: 1.2	Sugar: 1.7	Protein: 1.3

INGREDIENTS

- 2 zucchini, cut into sticks
- 1 tablespoon olive oil
- 1 teaspoon peppercorns, minced
- ½ teaspoon dried basil
- ¼ teaspoon chili flakes

Sweet and Sour Cucumber Rings

🕐 10 mins   🍲 15 mins   👤 4

INGREDIENTS

- ¼ cup fresh dill, chopped
- 3 English cucumbers, sliced
- ½ teaspoon ground black pepper
- 1 tablespoon olive oil
- 1 teaspoon Erythritol
- 1 tablespoon lemon juice

METHODS

O1   Put the sliced cucumbers in the bowl. Add fresh dill, ground black pepper, and olive oil.

O2   Add Erythritol and lemon juice. Stir the mixture well. Let the cucumbers marinate in the fridge for 15 minutes.

Nutritional Value

Calories: 73	Fat: 3.9	Carbs: 10.1
Fiber: 1.6	Sugar: 3.9	Protein: 2.1

INGREDIENTS

- 1/3 cup walnuts, chopped
- 2 zucchini
- 1 tablespoon olive oil
- ¼ cup water
- 1 oz Parmesan, grated

Zucchini Pasta

 15 mins 7 mins 4

METHODS

O1 Make the spirals from the zucchini with the help of the spiralizer. Preheat the olive oil and put the spiralized zucchini inside. Roast it for 1 minute.

O2 Add water and cook the pasta for 3 minutes more. Top the cooked zucchini pasta with Parmesan and walnuts.

Nutritional Value

Calories: 133	Fat: 11.4	Carbs: 4.6
Fiber: 1.8	Sugar: 1.8	Protein: 6

INGREDIENTS

- 1 oz pumpkin seeds
- 1 oz almonds, chopped
- 1-pound butternut squash
- 1 tablespoon olive oil
- 1 teaspoon ground cinnamon

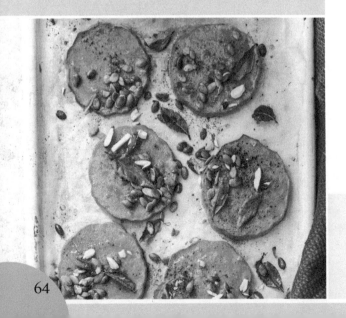

Aromatic Roasted Butternut Squash

 15 mins 40 mins 4

METHODS

O1 Cut the butternut squash into wedges and place on the baking tray.

O2 Sprinkle the butternut squash with pumpkin seeds, almonds, olive oil, and ground cinnamon. Bake the vegetable for 40 minutes at 350°F.

Nutritional Value

Calories: 162	Fat: 10.4	Carbs: 16.5
Fiber: 3.8	Sugar: 2.9	Protein: 4.4

Fall Style Mushrooms

 15 mins 80 mins 👧 4

METHODS

01 Pour olive oil into the pan and add onion. Roast the onion for 4 minutes or until light brown.

02 Place the cremini mushrooms in the pan and roast for 5 minutes. Stir the mushrooms well.

03 Sprinkle the mushrooms with ground black pepper and salt, stir them, then cook for 1 minute more. Garnish the cooked mushrooms with fresh parsley.

Nutritional Value

Calories: 139	Fat: 7.4	Carbs: 13.2
Fiber: 2.6	Sugar: 5.2	Protein: 6.5

INGREDIENTS

- 2-pounds cremini mushrooms, halved
- 1 yellow onion, diced
- 2 tablespoons olive oil
- 1 teaspoon ground black pepper
- ½ teaspoon salt
- 2 oz fresh parsley

Carrot French Fries

 15 mins 20 mins 👧 4

METHODS

01 Cut the carrots into French fried shapes and place them on a parchment-lined baking tray. Sprinkle carrots with ground coriander and olive oil.

02 Carefully mix the carrots and flatten them in one layer. Bake the carrot French fries for 20 minutes at 350°F.

Nutritional Value

Calories: 67	Fat: 3.5	Carbs: 8.9
Fiber: 2.2	Sugar: 4.4	Protein: 0.7

INGREDIENTS

- 5 big carrots, peeled
- 1 teaspoon ground coriander
- 1 tablespoon olive oil

INGREDIENTS

- 2 cups russet potatoes, roughly chopped
- ¼ cup fresh dill, chopped
- 1 tablespoon olive oil
- 1 teaspoon salt
- 3 cups water

Country Style Potatoes

 15 mins 20 mins 4

METHODS

01 Bring water to a boil and put potatoes inside. Boil the potatoes for 10 minutes. Cover the baking tray with parchment.

02 Drain the potatoes and transfer them to the prepared baking tray. Sprinkle the potatoes with olive oil and salt and broil in the oven for 10 minutes.

03 Add fresh dill to the cooked potato and gently mix.

Nutritional Value

Calories: 89   Fat: 3.7   Carbs: 13.5

Fiber: 2.2   Sugar: 0.9   Protein: 1.9

INGREDIENTS

- 4 big Russet potatoes
- 1 cup Mozzarella cheese, shredded
- 1 Roma tomato, diced
- 1 oz green onions, chopped

Kumpir

 15 mins 30 mins 4

METHODS

01 Put the potatoes in the oven and bake for 30 minutes at 375°F or until the potatoes are soft.

02 Peel the upper surface of the potatoes and mash the inside of the potato using a fork. This should create a potato boat with the skin intact. Combine cheese with tomato

03 Place some cheese mixture into each potato and gently stir until the cheese is melted. Then top each potato with the green onion.

Nutritional Value

Calories: 287   Fat: 1.8   Carbs: 61

Fiber: 9.5   Sugar: 5.7   Protein: 8.8

DESSERTS

INGREDIENTS

- ½ cup raspberries
- ½ cup blueberries
- ½ cup blackberries
- ½ cup strawberries, roughly chopped
- 2 cups Greek yogurt

Berries and Yogurt Bites

 15 mins   45 mins   4

METHODS

O1   Put the Greek yogurt in the big mixing bowl. Add all remaining ingredients and carefully combine. Take the big tray and transfer the mixture inside, flatten it well.

O2   Transfer the tray to the freezer and freeze until the mixture is solid (around 45 minutes).

O3   Remove the frozen yogurt mixture from the freezer and crack it into bites.

Nutritional Value

Calories: 240   Fat: 3.6   Carbs: 43.4

Fiber: 11   Sugar: 28.6   Protein: 13.6

INGREDIENTS

- 4 green apples
- ½ cup walnuts, chopped
- 1 tablespoon sugar, powdered
- 4 fresh mint leaves

Baked Apples

 15 mins   25 mins   4

METHODS

O1   Remove the core from the apples and put the walnuts inside. Place the apples on the baking tray and bake at 365°F for 25 minutes.

O2   Then sieve the powdered sugar over the apples and top them with mint leaves.

Nutritional Value

Calories: 229   Fat: 9.7   Carbs: 36.3

Fiber: 7.2   Sugar: 26.4   Protein: 4.7

Sweet Cherries Pie

🕐 15 mins 🍲 50 mins 👤 4

INGREDIENTS

- 1 cup all-purpose flour
- 1 cup sweet cherries
- 3 eggs, beaten
- ¼ cup Erythritol
- 1 teaspoon baking powder
- 1 teaspoon vanilla extract
- ¼ cup plain yogurt

METHODS

01 In the mixing bowl, combine plain yogurt with vanilla extract, baking powder, Erythritol, eggs, and flour until a homogeneous texture.

02 Add sweet cherries and stir gently. Pour the mixture into the baking pan and flatten the surface well.

03 Bake the pie at 350°F for 50 minutes. Let it cool down and cut it into servings.

Nutritional Value

Calories: 347   Fat: 3.9   Carbs: 67.6

Fiber: 1.8   Sugar: 1.5   Protein: 8.8

Almond Cake

🕐 15 mins 🍲 45 mins 👤 4

INGREDIENTS

- 1 cup carrot, grated
- 1 cup almond meal
- ⅓ cup all-purpose flour
- 1 teaspoon ground nutmeg
- 3 eggs, beaten
- ½ cup olive oil
- 1 tablespoon baking powder
- 1 tablespoon lemon juice

METHODS

01 In the mixing bowl, mix almond meal, all-purpose flour, ground nutmeg, eggs, olive oil, baking powder, and lemon juice.

02 When the mixture is smooth and homogeneous, add carrot and stir well. Transfer the cake mixture to the baking pan and flatten gently.

03 Bake the cake at 355°F for 45 minutes.

Nutritional Value

Calories: 457   Fat: 40.7   Carbs: 18.1

Fiber: 4.1   Sugar: 2.9   Protein: 10.5

INGREDIENTS

- 3 tablespoons coconut oil
- 1 cup all-purpose flour
- 1 teaspoon baking powder
- 1 egg, beaten
- 1 tablespoon lemon juice
- 1 cup plums, pitted, halved
- 3 tablespoons Erythritol

Plum Pie

 25 mins 45 mins 4

METHODS

O1 The dough: in the mixing bowl, mix coconut oil, flour, baking powder, egg, and lemon juice. Knead the dough until it reaches a non-sticky consistency.

O2 Cut the dough into 2 parts. Put one part of the dough in the freezer for 15 minutes. Put the first part of the dough in the baking pan and flatten it into the shape of the pie crust.

O3 Place the plums over the pie crust and sprinkle them with Erythritol. Grate the remaining dough over the plums. Bake the pie at 355°F for 45 minutes.

Nutritional Value

Calories: 227	Fat: 11.7	Carbs: 26.6
Fiber: 1.1	Sugar: 2	Protein: 4.8

INGREDIENTS

- 1 cup plain yogurt
- ½ cup cocoa powder
- 1 tablespoon baking powder
- 1 cup all-purpose flour
- 3 tablespoons olive oil
- ½ cup Erythritol
- 2 tablespoon coconut oil

Chocolate Cake

 15 mins 40 mins 4

METHODS

O1 Combine yogurt with baking powder, Erythritol, and flour. When the mixture is homogeneous add cocoa powder (leave out 1 tablespoon of cocoa powder for decoration). Stir the mixture until smooth.

O2 Pour the batter into the baking pan and bake at 350°F for 40 minutes.

O3 Mix coconut oil and the remaining cocoa powder. Whisk it well. When the cake is cooked, cool it well and top it with cocoa powder glaze.

Nutritional Value

Calories: 333	Fat: 19.8	Carbs: 35.8
Fiber: 4.1	Sugar: 4.6	Protein: 8.7

Lemon Pie

🕐 15 mins 🍲 45 mins 👤 6

METHODS

O1 Put all ingredients in the mixing bowl and mix until you get a smooth and homogeneous texture.

O2 Then pour the mixture into the baking pan and bake at 350°F for 45 minutes. Let the pie cool down, then cut it into servings.

Nutritional Value

Calories: 187   Fat: 11   Carbs: 17

Fiber: 0.7   Sugar: 0.8   Protein: 5.1

INGREDIENTS

- ½ cup lemon juice
- ¼ cup olive oil
- 1 teaspoon baking powder
- 3 eggs, beaten
- 1 cup all-purpose flour
- ⅓ cup Erythritol
- 1 teaspoon vanilla extract

Raspberries Pie

🕐 15 mins 🍲 45 mins 👤 4

METHODS

O1 In the mixing bowl, combine eggs with flour, Erythritol, olive oil, baking powder, and lemon juice. When the mixture is homogeneous, add raspberries, and gently stir.

O2 Pour the pie batter into the baking pan and bake at 360°F for 45 minutes. Let the cooked pie cool down and top with fresh raspberries.

Nutritional Value

Calories: 319   Fat: 18.6   Carbs: 28.6

Fiber: 2.9   Sugar: 1.9   Protein: 10.6

INGREDIENTS

- 5 eggs, beaten
- 1 cup all-purpose flour
- 1 cup raspberries
- ½ cup Erythritol
- ¼ cup olive oil
- 1 teaspoon baking powder
- 1 tablespoon lemon juice

INGREDIENTS

- ⅓ cup walnuts, chopped
- 1 cup sour cherries, pitted
- 2 eggs, beaten
- 1 cup plain yogurt
- 1 cup all-purpose flour
- ½ cup Erythritol
- 1 teaspoon vanilla extract
- 1 teaspoon baking soda

Sour Cherry Pie

 15 mins 50 mins 4

METHODS

01 Mix eggs with yogurt, flour, Erythritol, vanilla extract, and baking soda until smooth.

02 Add sour cherries and walnuts and gently stir the pie butter.

03 Pour the batter into the baking pan, flatten it gently, and bake at 355°F for 50 minutes. Let the pie cool down, then cut it into servings.

Nutritional Value

Calories: 427	Fat: 9.5	Carbs: 71.1
Fiber: 2.4	Sugar: 4.8	Protein: 12.6

INGREDIENTS

- 1 cup blueberries
- 1 cup Erythritol
- 1 teaspoon vanilla extract
- ½ cup ricotta cheese
- 2 whole-grain bagels, halved, toasted

Blueberries Brouschetta

 30 mins 20 mins 4

METHODS

01 Blend blueberries with Erythritol and vanilla extract (leave a few blueberries for decoration). Spread the bagel halves with ricotta cheese.

02 Then top it with blended blueberries and top with the remaining blueberries.

Nutritional Value

Calories: 374	Fat: 17.3	Carbs: 43.5
Fiber: 4.2	Sugar: 4.2	Protein: 11.4

Apple Tari

🕐 15 mins 🍲 40 mins 👤 4

METHODS

01 In the mixing bowl, combine flour with coconut oil, baking powder, and vanilla extract. Knead the dough until it reaches a non-sticky consistency.

02 Transfer the dough to the baking mold, flatten it to the shape of the pie crust, and bake for 10 minutes at 350°F.

03 Fill the pie crust with apples. Sprinkle the apples with ground cinnamon. Bake the pie for 30 minutes more at 360°F. Let the pie cool down, then cut it into servings.

Nutritional Value

Calories: 234   Fat: 3.4   Carbs: 50.5

Fiber: 6.1   Sugar: 23.4   Protein: 3.2

INGREDIENTS

- 5 granny Smith apples, sliced
- 1 tablespoon ground coriander
- 1 cup all-purpose flour
- 1 tablespoon coconut oil
- 1 teaspoon baking powder
- 1 teaspoon vanilla extract

Tender Pumpkin Bites

🕐 15 mins 🍲 30 mins 👤 4

METHODS

01 In the mixing bowl, combine Erythritol, ground cinnamon, ground coriander, and dried thyme. Rub the pumpkin wedges with the thyme mixture and place them on the baking tray.

02 Bake the pumpkin for 30 minutes at 350°F. Sprinkle the cooked pumpkin with pumpkin seeds.

Nutritional Value

Calories: 90   Fat: 1.7   Carbs: 19.1

Fiber: 6.9   Sugar: 7.5   Protein: 3.1

INGREDIENTS

- 2-pounds pumpkin, cut into wedges
- 1 tablespoon pumpkin seeds
- 1 teaspoon dried thyme
- 1 tablespoon Erythritol
- ½ teaspoon ground cinnamon
- ¼ teaspoon ground coriander

INGREDIENTS

- 2 mangoes, peeled, pitted, chopped
- I cup raspberries
- ½ cup blueberries
- ½ cup strawberries, chopped
- I teaspoon lemon juice
- ½ teaspoon liquid honey

Dessert Fruit Bowl

🕐 15 mins   🍲 0 mins   👤 4

METHODS

O1   Put mango, raspberries, strawberries, and blueberries in the salad bowl and gently mix.

O2   Sprinkle the mixture with liquid honey and lemon juice.

Nutritional Value

Calories: 136	Fat: 1	Carbs: 33.6
Fiber: 5.5	Sugar: 27.7	Protein: 2

INGREDIENTS

- I cup strawberries
- ½ cup blueberries
- ¼ cup Erythritol
- I cup plain yogurt
- I cup oatmeal

Berries Jars

🕐 15 mins   🍲 60 mins   👤 4

METHODS

O1   Blend strawberries with Erythritol. Put I teaspoon of strawberry blend in the bottom of the serving jar.

O2   Add yogurt and oatmeal. Repeat the steps till you use all ingredients.

O3   Then top the jars with blueberries and strawberries (if desired) and store the meal in the fridge for I hour.

Nutritional Value

Calories: 143	Fat: 2.3	Carbs: 23.6
Fiber: 3.2	Sugar: 8.1	Protein: 6.6

60-DAY MEAL PLAN

1600 calories Mediterranean Diet meal plan

DAY	BREAKFAST	LUNCH	SNACK	DINNER
1	Egg Wrap	Rice and Cheese Stuffed Peppers	Hummus	Lemon Seabream
2	Breakfast Scramble Potato Salad	Lemony Anchovies	Baked Apples Thyme Mackerel	Chicken Cutlets with Arugula and Tomatoes
3	Almond and Strawberries Oatmeal	Pesto Seabass	Red Cabbage and Pepper Salad	Roasted Rosemary Chicken Wings Caprese
4	Morning Chia Pudding	Creamy Mushrooms Fettuccini	Antipasto Skewers	Lemongrass Lobster
5	Tender Omelet with Cherry Tomatoes Greek Salad	Garlic Lamb on Rack	Blueberries Tart	Chicken Patties with Tomato Sauce
6	Breakfast Quiche	Parmesan and Spinach Rice	Tzatziki	Carrot and Lentils Bowl Whole Cornish Hens with Oranges
7	Menemen Tabbouleh Salad	Onion Chicken Thighs	Nachos with Mediterranean Dip	Spaghetti Bolognese
8	Shakshuka Zucchini Muffins	Pesto and Zucchini Pasta	Turkish Pide	Caprese
9	Beetroot Salad Fig Toast	Tender Bulgur with Tomatoes	Ciabatta Bites	Spring Radish Salad Sour Cherry Pie
10	Zucchini Pancakes Tender Omelet with Cherry Tomatoes	Tomato Ezme Arugula and Chicken Salad	Berries and Yogurt Bites	Bay Leaf and Onion Beef Bites Tender Brussel Sprouts Halves

DAY	BREAKFAST	LUNCH	SNACK	DINNER
11	Strawberries Smoothie Bowl	Garlic and Dill Shrimps	Apple Tart	Lemony Anchovies Berries Jars
12	Shakshuka White Beans Salad	Parmigiana and Tomatoes Pasta	Cheese and Pork Balls	Sweet Cherries Pie
13	Egg Wrap	Spaghetti Bolognese	Antipasto Skewers	Almond Cake
14	Basil Fried Egg Spinach and Chickpea Salad	Pesto and Zucchini Pasta	Pasta Salad	Plum Pie
15	Tender Omelet with Cherry Tomatoes	Seafood Spaghetti	Garlic Chicken Bites	Chocolate Cake
16	Breakfast Scramble Fine Bulgur Salad	Creamy Mushrooms Fettuccini	Spaghetti Bolognese	Raspberries Pie
17	Oatmeal and Carrot Muffins Red Cabbage and Pepper Salad	Carrot and Lentils Bowl	Chicken Wings in Tomato Sauce	Sour Cherry Pie
18	Zucchini Pancakes Spring Radish Salad	Tender Bulgur with Tomatoes Menemen	Tzatziki	Lasagna Berries Jars
19	Breakfast Quiche Beetroot Salad	Lemon and Herbs Couscous	Antipasto Skewers	Blueberries Tart
20	Breakfast Bowl	Almond and Strawberries Oatmeal	Eggplant Ragout	Turkish Pide
21	Fig Toast Chopped Salad	Rice and Cheese Stuffed Peppers	Fall Style Mushrooms	Basil Chicken Drumsticks Plum Pie
22	Strawberries Smoothie Bowl Chopped Salad	Beef Rice	Bay Leaf and Onion Beef Bites	Basil and Tomato Meatballs
23	Menemen Arugula and Chicken Salad	Smoked Sausages and Vegetable Rice	Greek Salad Thyme Mackerel	Garlic Lamb on Rac

DAY	BREAKFAST	LUNCH	SNACK	DINNER
24	Banana Crepes	Parmesan and Spinach Rice	Potato Salad	Grilled Trout Stuffed with Vegetables
25	Morning Chia Pudding	Carrot and Lentils Bowl	Bruschetta with Dried Tomatoes	Sweet and Sour Bacon Plum Pie
26	Egg Wrap	Rice and Cheese Stuffed Peppers	Hummus	Lemon Seabream
27	Shakshuka	Pesto and Zucchini Pasta Zucchini Muffins	Turkish Pide	Caprese
28	Summer Salad Bay Leaf and Onion Beef Bites	Broiled Salmon	Potato Salad	Lasagna
29	Greek Salad Oatmeal and Carrot Muffins	Eggless Crème Brule	Caprese	Onion Chicken Thighs
30	Light Caesar	Spiced Seabass with Cherry Tomatoes	Ciabatta Bites Rice in Wine Leaves	Nachos with Mediterranean Dip Spring Radish Salad
31	Arugula and Chicken Salad	Lemon Seabream	Stuffed Zucchini Flowers	Antipasto Skewers Mustard Chicken Drumsticks
32	Tender Omelet with Cherry Tomatoes	Seafood Spaghetti	Garlic Chicken Bites	Chocolate Cake
33	Spinach and Chickpea Salad	Pesto Seabass Fall Style Mushrooms	Tender Brussel Sprouts Halves	Parmigiana and Tomatoes Pasta
34	White Beans Salad	Tender Mussel Shells	Zucchini and Corn Pie	Vegetable Gratin Hummus
35	Light Caesar	Tender Mackerel Cooked in Foil	Aromatic Roasted Butternut Squash	Mustard Chicken Drumsticks
36	Banana Crepes	Grilled Trout Stuffed with Vegetables	Fall Style Mushrooms	Basil Chicken Drumsticks

DAY	BREAKFAST	LUNCH	SNACK	DINNER
37	Banana Crepes	Lemony Anchovies	Kumpir	Vegetable Gratin Carrot and Lentils Bowl
38	Morning Chia Pudding	Lemony Sardines	Vegetable Gratin	Light Caesar
39	Strawberries Smoothie Bowl	Piri Piri Shrimps	Tzatziki Beetroot Salad	Basil and Tomato Meatballs
40	White Beans Salad	Garlic and Dill Shrimps	Chocolate Cake	Garlic Lamb on Rack
41	Breakfast Quiche	Basil Chicken Drumsticks	Eggplant Ragout	Bay Leaf and Onion Beef Bites
42	Oatmeal and Carrot Muffins	Onion Chicken Thighs	Zucchini Pancakes	Sweet and Sour Bacon
43	Tender Omelet with Cherry Tomatoes	Chicken Wings in Tomato Sauce	Garlic and Dill Shrimps	Lasagna
44	Egg Wrap Almond and Strawberries Oatmeal	Mustard Chicken Drumsticks		Turkish Pide
45	Sweet Cherries Pie	Chicken Cutlets with Arugula and Tomatoes	Nachos with Mediterranean Dip Berries and Yogurt Bites	Rosemary Meatloaf Chopped Salad
46	Almond Cake	Chicken Patties with Tomato Sauce	Hummus Rice in Wine Leaves	Cheese and Pork Balls Zucchini Muffins
47	Chocolate Cake	Roasted Rosemary Chicken Wings	Strawberries Smoothie Bowl	Garlic Chicken Bite
48	Beetroot Salad Fig Toast	Tender Bulgur with Tomatoes	Ciabatta Bites	Spring Radish Sala Sour Cherry Pie
49	Basil Fried Egg Spinach and Chickpea Salad	Pesto and Zucchini Pasta	Pasta Salad	Plum Pie

DAY	BREAKFAST	LUNCH	SNACK	DINNER
50	Summer Salad Bay Leaf and Onion Beef Bites	Broiled Salmon	Potato Salad	Lasagna
51	Greek Salad Oatmeal and Carrot Muffins	Eggless Crème Brule	Caprese	Onion Chicken Thighs
52	Breakfast Bowl	Almond and Strawberries Oatmeal	Eggplant Ragout	Turkish Pide
53	Strawberries Smoothie Bowl	Piri Piri Shrimps	Tzatziki Beetroot Salad	Basil and Tomato Meatballs
54	Strawberries Smoothie Bowl	Garlic and Dill Shrimps	Apple Tart	Lemony Anchovies Berries Jars
55	Almond and Strawberries Oatmeal	Pesto Seabass	Red Cabbage and Pepper Salad	Roasted Rosemary Chicken Wings Caprese
56	Tender Omelet with Cherry Tomatoes Greek Salad	Garlic Lamb on Rack	Blueberries Tart	Chicken Patties with Tomato Sauce
57	Oatmeal and Carrot Muffins Red Cabbage and Pepper Salad	Carrot and Lentils Bowl	Chicken Wings in Tomato Sauce	Sour Cherry Pie
58	Strawberries Smoothie Bowl Chopped Salad	Beef Rice	Bay Leaf and Onion Beef Bites	Basil and Tomato Meatballs
59	Banana Crepes	Parmesan and Spinach Rice	Potato Salad	Grilled Trout Stuffed with Vegetables
60	Breakfast Quiche Beetroot Salad	Lemon and Herbs Couscous	Antipasto Skewers	Blueberries Tart

MEASUREMENT CONVERSION CHARTS

CUP	OUNCES	MILLILITERS	TABLESPOONS
1/16 CUPS	1/2 OZ	15 ML	1 TBSP
1/8 CUPS	1 OZ	30 ML	3 TBSP
1/4 CUPS	2 OZ	59 ML	4 TBSP
1/3 CUPS	2.5 OZ	79 ML	5.5 TBSP
3/8 CUPS	3 OZ	90 ML	6 TBSP
1/2 CUPS	4 OZ	118 ML	8 TBSP
2/3 CUPS	5 OZ	158 ML	11 TBSP
3/4 CUPS	6 OZ	177 ML	12 TBSP
1 CUPS	8 OZ	240 ML	16 TBSP
2 CUPS	16 OZ	480 ML	32 TBSP
4 CUPS	32 OZ	960 ML	64 TBSP
5 CUPS	40 OZ	1180 ML	80 TBSP
6 CUPS	48 OZ	1420 ML	96 TBSP
8 CUPS	64 OZ	1895 ML	128 TBSP

MEASUREMENT

IMPERIAL	METRIC
1/2 OZ	15 G
1 OZ	29 G
2 OZ	57 G
3 OZ	85 G
4 OZ	113 G
5 OZ	141 G
6 OZ	170 G
8 OZ	227 G
10 OZ	283 G
12 OZ	340 G
13 OZ	369 G
14 OZ	397 G
15 OZ	425 G
1 LB	453 G

WEIGHT

FAHRENHEIT	CELSIUS
100 °F	37 °C
150 °F	65 °C
200 °F	93 °C
250 °F	121 °C
300 °F	150 °C
325 °F	160 °C
350 °F	180 °C
375 °F	190 °C
400 °F	200 °C
425 °F	220 °C
450 °F	230 °C
500 °F	260 °C
525 °F	274 °C
550 °F	288 °C

TEMPERATURE

Mediterranean Diet Pyramid

Red meats & sweets
Enjoy Sparingly

Poultry, eggs & dairy
Enjoy 1-2x/wk

Fish, seafood & omega-3 rich foods
Enjoy >3x/wk

Whole grains, legumes, fruit, vegetables, healthy fats, herbs & spices
Enjoy Daily

Physical activity, meal & family time
Enjoy Daily

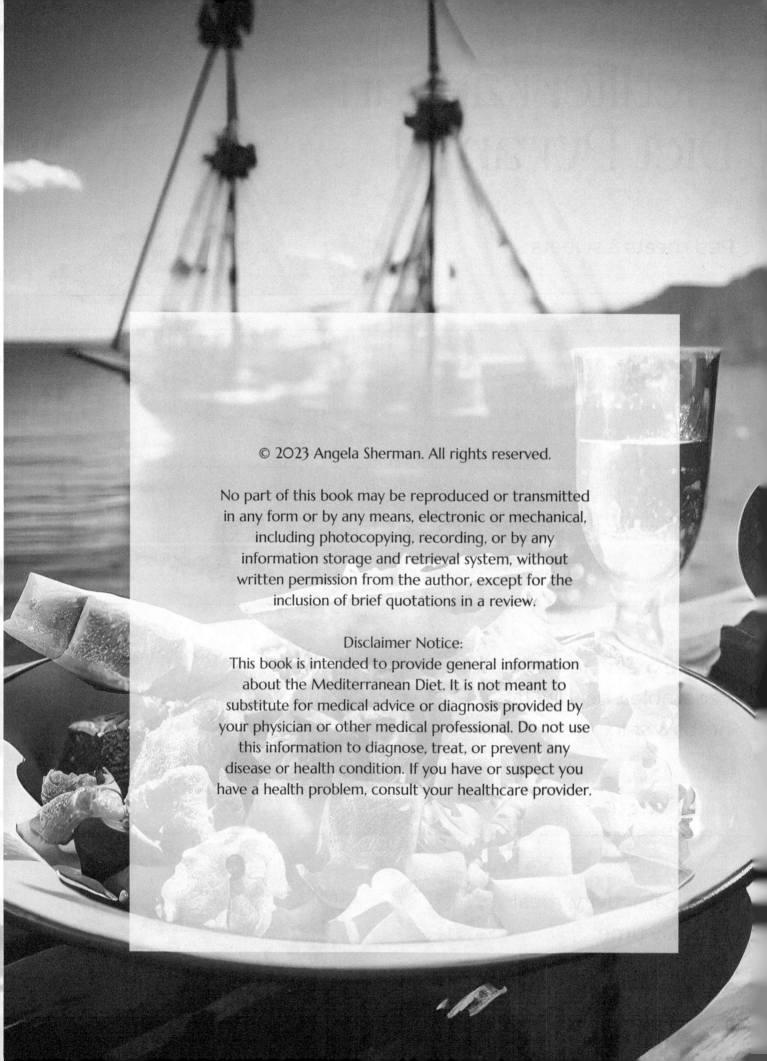

Disclaimer Notice:
This book is intended to provide general information about the Mediterranean Diet. It is not meant to substitute for medical advice or diagnosis provided by your physician or other medical professional. Do not use this information to diagnose, treat, or prevent any disease or health condition. If you have or suspect you have a health problem, consult your healthcare provider.

Made in the USA
Las Vegas, NV
15 April 2024

88691247R00046